For Sue
with affection

In Spite of All

from

Lois

Offord

Dec 2023

Luís Amorim de Sousa

In Spite of All

a memoir of
Alberto de Lacerda

Shearsman Books

Published in the United Kingdom in 2015 by
Shearsman Books
50 Westons Hill Drive, Emersons Green, Bristol BS16 7DF

Shearsman Books Ltd Registered Office
30–31 St. James Place, Mangotsfield, Bristol BS16 9JB
(this address not for correspondence)

www.shearsman.com

ISBN 978-1-84861-363-8

ACKNOWLEDGEMENTS
Poems by Alberto de Lacerda quoted in this book are reprinted
by permission of the Estate of Alberto de Lacerda.

Special words of gratitude for their generous, wise and constructive
comments are due to John McEwen, John Sims and Anthony Rudolf
who were Alberto de Lacerda's friends. The same words are extended to
James Maynard and David Whittaker who were too late to meet him
but are now part of the circle.

To Paula Rego and Samuel Lock, for their friendship and their drawings.

To John McEwen once more and my son João
for all their help at a difficult time.

To London, beloved city.

To Mary, for everything.

COVER
Front: Alberto de Lacerda by Paula Rego, 2002,
copyright Paula Rego, by courtesy of Marlborough Fine Art, London.
Back: Alberto's room in Tite Street, by Samuel Lock, 1970,
copyright © Samuel Lock.

All photographs in the book have been drawn from the estate of
Alberto de Lacerda. The photos on pp. 96 and 111 are
copyright © Alberto Vourvoulias-Bush and Richard Roberts,
respectively, and are reproduced here with permission.

Oh Life, be beautiful!

Alberto de Lacerda – Diary entry 19-12-1951,
on board the *Andes*, facing Southampton.

Introduction

In 1959, aged 21, I left Lourenço Marques, the colonial capital of Mozambique, to live in freedom and be a poet in London. I arrived with two addresses. The first of these was of a place to stay. The second, I very much hoped, would lead me to the presence of the Portuguese poet Alberto de Lacerda.

Alberto had lived in London for a number of years, worked for the BBC, and was the author of a famous book, his first, published by Allen & Unwin. To have a literary debut in England, to have one's poems appear in a bilingual edition and, furthermore, introduced and co-translated by a famous literary figure, was – to me – quite unimaginable. The book was *77 Poems*. Its patron was Arthur Waley, and the critics praised it highly.

It loomed large in my mind that Alberto came from Mozambique. The experience of colonial life in Africa under the Salazar regime, common acquaintances in the town where both of us had grown up, and most importantly, the Portuguese language, would lead me straight, so I thought, into Alberto's world. I looked forward to his friendship, his guidance and his advice. As it turned out, I was right.

It took me a while to find him. Alberto had moved from his old address in Chelsea, spent a few months in Brazil and suffered a hip fracture in Lisbon from which he would never entirely recover. Alberto was left with a limp.

We met in a King's Road café in 1961. Alberto asked me what I had been doing and listened most intently while I talked. I told him of my visits to galleries and bookshops, to pubs where live jazz was played, of my new found love of the Thames and its bridges, of wonderful book dealers where I was allowed to leaf through first editions of the modern classics. I told him all of that. Without knowing it I was describing his own personal way of life. We became friends right away.

Soon after that first encounter, Alberto and I were doing our explorations side by side. During those outings I also became a witness to his compulsive collecting: records, books, and works of art, things that brought him close to people whom he admired, and also places and creative movements from which he took both pleasure and inspiration. He did it without a penny to his name, in true bohemian fashion. His needs were not acquisitive. He was creating a world. His world. His own and very private treasure island.

We remained friends to the end. Alberto's reputation as a poet took him to the United States as a Visiting Professor. He held positions in Austin, in New York, and most sustainedly in Boston. Following the Carnation Revolution that brought democracy back to Portugal in 1974, I was invited and took a diplomatic posting at the Embassy of Portugal in Washington D.C.

Alberto and I were in the same country again. We visited each other as much as we could, met in New York to see major exhibitions, and talked assiduously by phone.

He was a wonderful communicator and a great reader of poetry. I took professional advantage of his exceptional gifts and found him cultural engagements as frequently as I could. That job was not always easy, as Alberto maintained extremely high standards that on occasion could prove difficult to meet. The most impressive of those public engagements was his reading, the first by a Portuguese poet, at the Library of Congress.

Later, a couple of diplomatic transfers brought me to London again, after Alberto had retired. Throughout his lecturing years he never abandoned London. London was his true refuge. After many, many years, Alberto and I were both in London again.

However, his stays abroad, his age, the disappearance of friends and familiar places, weighed on him. He became testier and more solitary. My work in London did not allow me the freedom that I had enjoyed in earlier days. We saw each other as frequently as we could and talked on the telephone most days.

As always. No matter where we were living. He often joked that our friendship "was becoming electronic." He also solemnly said: "friendship is a concrete thing."

He was the most exciting, most exacting, most exceptional, most exemplary of friends.

The rest is told in this book.

Alberto in Sloane Square, 1952.

1

There was a recorded message on our phone. It was a message from Jill. Jill McEwen. John's wife.

"Terrible news, I'm afraid. Alberto was found in a coma. John is with him at the hospital!"

"I have to go to London!" I said. Mary guessed it right away.

"It is Alberto, isn't it?"

"He is dying. I have to go."

We were living in Cascais. There were urgent calls to be made, there was a ticket to buy, a suitcase to be packed, an airport cab to be called. We did it all in a rush. And then I said:

"Where's the key?"

"The key? What key?" asked Mary.

"The key to Alberto's safe. He's got a box at the bank. I really hope not to need it but he kept talking about it. It's all written there, he said. I better go get that key."

"What's written there?"

"His wishes, in case he dies. He asked me quite a few times to take care of all his writings. But he never really told me what to do. He simply said that his wishes are kept there, inside that box, and sent me a key, remember? I'd better go fetch it now."

The cab was on its way.

"Please hold the cab if it comes. First I have to get that key." I had seen it recently. And now I scrambled to find it.

"Where the devil is that key? I've always kept it right here. It's just a flat little thing in a blue-grey envelope… one of Alberto's, you know?…"

A Basildon Bond envelope. Alberto's favourite stationery. And Mary:

"There's your cab! Shall I go tell it to wait and help you look for that key?"

"Never mind. We'll find it later. I hope it won't be needed. I really hope that he makes it. I'd better be going now. I will call you later from London. I'll call as soon as I can. Poor Alberto!"

We gave each other a hug. An anxious hug. Things felt bad.

2

Things had not been right for Alberto even before we left London. He neglected his appearance and became testier than usual. He protested about noise pollution, urban change, lack of civility. He protested above all about music in restaurants. That was his pet complaint. It came from a music lover.

"Nobody is listening," he said. "They are just producing noise and destroying conversation." He complained about discomfort, and in less guarded moments, alluded to loneliness.

When I reached retirement age Mary and I opted to live in Cascais. My pension was insufficient to meet expenses in London. We had a flat by the sea. We had a child to bring up. Life would be easier in Portugal. Cascais is a lovely place. I felt uneasy about leaving. Leaving London and Alberto. But a decision was needed and a decision was taken.

Alberto was most unhappy with that. He made it quite plain to me.

"What on earth will you be doing there? This is your city. Why leave it? Why leave it now?" I tried in vain to explain. Nothing doing. Alberto would not be convinced.

"But there is nothing for you there! This is where your friends are."

Then, adding a personal note, he said that he had imagined that as I got more free time I would find it a lot easier to join him more leisurely in his wanderings around London. Around "what is left of London."

He meant museums, galleries, bookshops, favourite places. We had done a lot of wandering in the past.

"And now, you want to go back."

He made a resigned expression and exclaimed:

"A pity, really, a pity… from now on our old friendship will be restricted to the occasional phone call."

I didn't know what to say. I mumbled something like "nonsense," and he added:

"You know very well my horror of machines. But thank goodness for the phone. At least, we can stay in touch!"

Alberto's often repeated strong dislike of all machines excluded his Kodak Brownie, his ancient record player and his disc-dialing phone. Outdated and precarious as they were, they met essential necessities. They helped him live and remember.

3

Alberto always lived alone. He was a man of routines. He left his flat in the morning and spent the day by himself. Unless he had an event or performance to attend, he usually came home for dinner. A healthy dinner, by his own description, that he prepared without fuss. It was preferably at night that he telephoned his friends. He called me regularly.

Everyone knew when he rang.

"Quick! The phone! It's Alberto!" It invariably was.

He let it ring a few times and if his call was not taken right away he put the receiver down and tried again.

"Hello! Were you watching television?"

"No, Alberto. I was in another room."

"Are you sure? I hear voices."

"Yes! It's Mary and Miguel. They are just talking."

"Ah!"

Whatever the circumstances, his exclamations were anything but ambiguous.

"Could you go back to that other room? The voices are disconcerting."

He required full attention to the things he had to say. In return he also listened with filtering concentration. His responses, often humorous, were spontaneous and sincere. His conversation was peppered with impressions of his outings, the people he had encountered, the letters he had received, and things remembered and seen, revealing a fecund world of discoveries and connections. His voice was full of inflexions, his narratives always compelling. A high level of proximity was expected from his calls.

"You are not speaking very clearly. Can you talk into the mouthpiece?... That's better! I love clarity. What were you saying just now?"

His calls were generally long. His farewells were prolonged.

"I had something else to add..." Then, a pause.

"Well! It's gone... When are you coming to London?"

"Soon, I hope. I will let you know, of course!"

"Do give me plenty of warning. There are things that I would love to see with you. Do you know what they are showing at the Tate?"

The Tate was the Tate Britain. He detested the Tate Modern, "a factory, not a museum!" His Tate was the old Tate. Not as important as the National Gallery, "nothing could possibly be," but it had "all those incomparable Turners" and the memory of so many eye-opening exhibitions. Supreme among all those, "the glory of the Picasso retrospective," the first to be held in London, curated by Roland Penrose, in 1961. And now the Tate, his Tate Gallery, had also acquired paintings by some of his artist friends. Among them Paula Rego. Every time her name came up he always said: "I adore her!"

Such were his chats on the phone. And with his farewells, his urgings:

"I have to go, now. Wonderful to hear your voice. And keep in touch. Don't go missing. And do write. Please write. You never write. Do write!"

And then, a tiny pause.

"Bye!"

He had a special way of saying bye. His vowels soared, crystal clear, lingered up there with an echo, and then trailed with a whisper. *Byyye!*

With Paula Rego, New York, 1983.

4

In spite of his reprimands, I did write to Alberto but, much more often, I called. Coming home one summer evening from a walk by the sea front, I called Alberto. It was our usual time. I found it strange that he did not take my call. The phone kept ringing and ringing. Alberto did not respond. This went on for two or three, a few consecutive days. And then his number went dead. I requested a test on his home number and the operator said:

"That number is discontinued."

I sent Alberto a note and called John, who confirmed the information. Alberto could not be reached. I waited for a response to the note that I had sent him. No response came from Alberto. I reached a fretting stage. And one day my phone rang and there he was. Alberto's voice sounded shrill and there was some background noise. Traffic noise.

"I'm calling you from the street. I am going to be brief. I am surrounded by diabolical noise. My home phone is out of order. Will you be coming to London? Send me a line. Bye!"

That was not his usual *bye*. It sounded anguished and rushed. It was troubling to think that Alberto would not be able to make or take calls at home. And I knew that he would not have his old telephone replaced. No more chats and divagations. The loss of that telephone was like a death in the family. He would refuse a mobile. He hated them with a passion. The dead phone was *his* phone. And it was dead. I could only write to him. He did not always respond. I started to get his news from John McEwen.

5

Alberto maintained lasting friendships with different members of the McEwen family. John was the youngest. Alberto met him in Scotland where his family had their home. Alberto was there as a guest to spend Christmas with them. To Alberto's great delight, John became an art critic with the *Sunday Telegraph*. Alberto never read the *Telegraph* but he bought it without fail when it carried John's reviews. They became assiduous friends. They enjoyed their time together, going to see art exhibitions and sharing personal memories of people, places, their London.

From time to time Alberto announced his intention to introduce me to John. He announced it frequently over a period of years. John was equally informed of the very same intention. But Alberto's introductions were not casual and even less, accidental. They were most carefully staged. The place, the date, his own mood, were factors to be considered. He introduced friends to friends in the hope of lasting friendships. And his friendships, as he put it, were "contagious."

With John McEwen, 2000.

6

My introduction to John took place at the Victoria and Albert Museum. We met for lunch in the cafeteria. Alberto loved museum cafeterias. He retreated there to write or for a rest while visiting exhibitions. He enjoyed their atmosphere and the discrete opportunity of having his kind of lunch: usually a cup of coffee with a tiny splash of milk, and a dry cake or a scone. Most museum cafeterias offered two further advantages: enough chairs to receive all his accoutrements, and the rarely missed opportunity of harvesting packets of sugar, always demerara sugar, from empty neighbouring tables. "Much healthier," he insisted.

There was a ritual to his getting settled. His chair had to be placed at exactly the right angle. Following that operation, his belongings were spread on two additional chairs that he dragged to chosen spots, to his right and to his left, both within his easy reach. His inseparable belongings consisted of a fur hat, a black parka, an incredibly long scarf, and a plastic shopping bag. On rainy days, he brought a spiky umbrella that looked like a witch's broom turned upside down. His inseparable plastic bag contained a coin purse, writing paper, a Bic pen (black ink, fine point), two newspapers (*The Times* and the *Evening Standard*) postage stamps, music programmes, assorted paper napkins from assorted coffee houses, always one book, letters, poems. Sometimes, from inside the bag he produced a little treasure, often a drawing or print sent by an artist friend.

"I just got this in the mail. Just like this... inside a letter. Can you imagine the danger? It could have been lost... or damaged! Can you imagine?..."

He had a favourite table in each different cafeteria. From there he moved to the shop. Alberto could not resist museum shops. He browsed through catalogues and reproduction post-cards that he always bought in duplicate: one to keep and one to send. He never sent the same card to more than one of his friends. Each friend got a different card.

John and I had long been contaminated by Alberto's common friendship. Genuine empathy predated our long announced introduction. Flying from Lisbon to London my mind was spinning with recollections and thoughts about Alberto's condition.

7

The cab driver who took me from the Heathrow Express out of Paddington Station kept talking all the way. My destination was the Chelsea and Westminster Hospital. That is where Alberto was.

"Did you have a pleasant journey, sir? Where did you arrive from? Portugal? Oh! Nice. Never been there myself, mind you, not yet. The "All-garv," right? I love the sea. Is this your first time in London? No? Oh you will notice a few changes. Quite a few changes, I'd say. You can't believe how many foreigners live here, now. Do you know this part of town? Bloody expensive, it is. Ridiculous, if you ask me. And why the hospital, sir? Are you seeing someone sick?"

"Yes, a friend. A very old friend of mine."

And there we were, at the entrance. I thought of Mary, waiting for news in Cascais. My cab driver was smiling. He took his fare and was pleased when I refused any change.

"Thank you guv! Cheers! God bless! I hope your friend is all right. And don't you worry too much. He'll feel better when he sees you. All the best! Cheers!"

I walked into the hospital. It was eerily empty. I found my bearings and went to the ominously called Acute Medical Unit.

"I've come to see Mr Alberto de Lacerda. I have just arrived from abroad. Can I see him now, please? How is he? If I have to wait, I will."

The duty nurse asked my name, looked at some papers, told me to wait just a minute and went to fetch someone else. A large, blond, smiley woman came towards me. I took her smile as a good sign. She looked like a senior nurse.

"Hello, Mr de Sousa. How are you, dear, OK? You are here to see Mr de Lacerda, right? Just follow me, please."

We went past a few patients, most of them seemingly asleep, and then she intoned:

"Al-ber-too! Your friend is here to see you. Mr de Sousa. I will leave you two together!" I murmured a "thank you nurse" and turning to me, she whispered: "We are keeping an eye on him. He's quite stable."

8

It was a small, open room. Everything in it looked efficient and clean. A monitor screen displayed a graph of fast moving green lights. The screen was next to his bed. There was a curious sound of heavy breathing. A strange, repetitive sound. That sound came from Alberto. He was lying very still with a breathing mask in place covering his nose and his mouth. His eyes were shut. He wore a hospital gown. He looked incredibly small. As usual, he was alone.

He was attached to a drip. I leaned over and took his hand very gently. His hand felt bony and dry. There was no response from Alberto. Just that weird sound of breathing through the mask.

"Alberto, it's me, Luís! I heard that you were unwell and I came over to see you. I'm here, now. We are in Chelsea, your Chelsea."

Delusion may have occurred. It most certainly did. But I had the strangest feeling that he heard me. I cannot describe a motion, any sign of recognition. There were none. Nothing that I could describe. Just a feeling. Something similar to what happens when you know what someone is thinking without a word being said. Not a murmur. Not a quiver. I looked again at the monitor. That constantly moving graph. No alteration. No change. I turned my eyes to Alberto. I found him a little thinner and so small, so very small. I pulled a chair, stroked his hand and started talking to him. I told him that I was writing a new book. Another book of memoirs. My American memoirs. I had brought some notes with me and read extracts from the sections where he is mentioned. They had to do with visiting museums. Memorable visits, all. Every single one of them. And softly, trying to speak as clearly as emotion would permit, I started to reminisce.

"Do you remember, Alberto, the Ginevra? *Ginevra de' Benci*. Do you remember how surprised you were to see it in the National Gallery, on your first visit to Washington? Do you remember, that? What exclamations you made. You didn't know it was there. And then you talked about the other Leonardo, the *Lady with the Ermine,* in Poland—is it in Poland?—and wondered which of the two would be the best. You said, 'This is unfair because none of us has seen the other painting. And here we are, and this is a masterpiece. But the other one,' you said, '…those eyes, the hand on the ermine, the contrast between the shyness and the sweetness of the lady and the latent ferocity of the ermine…' Do you remember that? And what about the Picassos in the new East Wing building—*The Saltimbanques,* the *Lady with a Fan…*—You said, 'What a great privilege!' You were surprised with all those lovely museums. And what about the Bonnard exhibition at the Phillips? That garden, that large one, full of tones of green and orange and crimson, do you remember? Bonnard painted lots of gardens, but you really took to that one. When you saw it, you stood still in front of it, you stood still for quite a while, there were tears in your eyes, and then you said: 'Paradise!' I never forgot that moment…"

Yes, you were quite surprised with Washington. You said it over and over. The bookshops and the museums. But, talking about museums, what about the great surprise of the Costakis Collection in New York? The ramps of the Guggenheim accelerated the heart as we came face to face with all those wonderful Russians. You loved the sound of their names, Popova, Rozanova, Gontcharova. Remember us writing poems, after that? Having a drink at the bar of that hotel, that one you like, what is it called?… never mind, you know the one… and there we were, writing poems. Writing poems in a frenzy. New York did it, I know! Wonderful city, New York! O'Hara city! You must get well, Alberto. Please make an effort. Do you remember that poem by Frank O'Hara about Lana Turner collapsing? I think it is in the *Lunch Poems.* At the end O'Hara writes *we love you, Lana Turner, get up.* That is what you have to do, Alberto. Please get well, get up!"

A different nurse came for me. She told me softly:

"Excuse me sir! The doctor would like to see you."

She was not smiling, I noticed. I patted Alberto's hand, told him that I would be back and followed her.

With Luís Amorim de Sousa and Mário Cesariny,
Tite Street, London, 1964.

9

The doctor was a young woman. She shook my hand and asked me to sit down. The nurse sat next to me. None of them smiled. They were both young and attractive. The doctor had Indian features. She was actually quite beautiful. She asked me how I was feeling.

"I would really like to know about my friend…"

She paused and rubbed her forehead very slowly. She pulled back a strand of hair that seemed to have been caught in her eyelashes. She had long, dark eyelashes. There was a clock on the wall showing meaningless time.

"I see that Mr de Lacerda does not seem to have a next of kin. Mr McEwen was here at the hospital and said that you would be coming from abroad. Are you related at all?"

"Yes, in a thousand ways, but not by family links… Will he live?"

The nurse asked me if I wanted a cup of tea. She placed her hand on my arm. I shook my head.

"No, thank you." Tears rolled.

"Your friend will not recover," said the doctor. The nurse's hand stroked my arm.

"You see, your friend suffered both a heart attack and a stroke. I understand that he was alone and was left unattended for a considerable period of time. Luckily Mr McEwen arranged to have him brought to the hospital. There was not much we could do. But he is not suffering. He may remain like this for days or just let go. He may die at any moment."

She paused again and looked straight into my eyes.

"I am very sorry, sir. Do go home. You look tired. If anything happens, we will tell you. Leave us a contact number. You can come back in the morning."

She stood up and shook my hand once again. The nurse asked me if I needed anything.

"No thank you, nurse. I'll be fine."

The doctor said "I'm so sorry!" And then the nurse asked politely: "Excuse me, sir. Excuse me for asking but… who is Mr de Lacerda?" My face was covered in tears. My voice was barely audible.

"A prince!" I said.

10

I went back to Alberto's bedside. No change. The same stillness, the same strange breathing noise through the mask. But it was him. It was Alberto. For a second, just a second, I half expected him to sit up, remove the mask, and say "how wonderful to see you" in his inimitable voice. Now that I had been told the bitter facts I was left without knowing what to do. I talked to him, again.

"Sorry, Alberto! I just stepped out for a minute."

I made an effort to keep my voice as close to normal as possible.

"Well! It is getting a bit late. I don't want to exhaust you with my talking. I have a flat where I'll stay. I'll have the place to myself. Nobody is there at the moment... Not that I need the whole flat. But anyway... I will go home now, and come back tomorrow morning. I'll buy *The Times* on the way and read you a column or two. You always enjoy the letters to the editor. We will have a look at those and we will see what else it brings. Does this sound like a good plan?"

It was extremely hard not to succumb to emotion. I looked at the monitor once again. No alteration. The same. The same little green lights tracing the very same graph.

Little green lights. I thought of traffic lights and the perils of crossing streets with Alberto. His total disregard of basic pedestrian rules made it a heart stopping experience. Whether ignoring or taking full advantage of his limp, he launched into a hair-raising zigzag through buses, cars, motorbikes, claiming that he had "a contract with the traffic," and crossed the streets with impunity. Once on the other side he resumed his strolling pace.

The first nurse came again to check him up. She looked larger. She verified his drip, took his pulse, glanced at the monitor screen, gave me a wave and a smile and went away. I leaned over Alberto and kissed him on the forehead.

"I'm going now, Alberto. See you tomorrow. Sleep well." It was the last time I saw him.

11

My son João was waiting for me at the flat. He gave me something to eat and a very welcome drink. I felt most dreadfully tired. I called Mary in Cascais, and John in London. They were both waiting for news. John and I compared impressions. He had been told just the same about Alberto's condition. I gave John the house number and that of a mobile phone that João had brought for me. We made plans to see each other in the morning. Mary and I talked for longer. I told her all that had happened since Cascais. She listened, asked a few questions, and then said: "I've been looking for that key... I can't find it anywhere. Can you think where it might be?"

Suddenly, that little key became an issue. Alberto was not going to recover. His wishes had to be respected. His things had to be kept safe. His writings had to be gathered. I absolutely had to know what he wanted me to do. This was a crisis. The thought of him being dead was inconceivable. Alberto had always been so full of life. And now his life ebbed away in that white hospital room.

João insisted that I went to bed. I did and fell right away into a deep, seamless sleep. Something like slipping an arm into a sleeve. And suddenly the phone rang. I looked at the time. Eight twenty. It was John.

"Luís," he said, "we have lost him. Alberto died in the night. The people at the hospital tried to call you. They rang you a couple of times. They could not reach you and called here. Dear Alberto! I feel so deeply sorry!"

I did not really grasp it right away. My first reaction was to apologize.

"I did not hear the phone, John. I am so sorry. When did they call? I'm so sorry. I did not hear a thing!..."

And then it hit me. Alberto had died. He was dead. There was a moment of silence.

"Are you there, John?... I'm so sorry. So very deeply sorry. I just don't know what to think!..."

But beyond my sense of loss, a thought did come to my mind. When somebody told Alberto that Ezra Pound had died, he said:

"A great tree has fallen!"

And he cried. Alberto's admiration for the poet won over his strong dislike of Pound's politics. A fallen tree. That was the thought on my mind. But I could not cry, not yet. Alberto was still too present to be mourned. I could hear John's breathing on the other side of the line. I looked around me. And suddenly, the whole room became a stage. I felt alone on that stage. And that was an overpowering and unexpected sensation.

With Christopher Middleton,
The Embankment, London, 1961

John and I arranged to meet at an old café in Hampstead. We both needed to let Alberto go. His loss was poignant. We needed a simple ritual. A farewell through common bonds. There is a moment in grief when words carry the occasion. Most of Alberto's old friends had been dead for quite a while. He used to say frequently that he was "a walking cemetery." Both John and I had been witness to quite a few of his losses. And to his splendid rewards. We had stories to exchange. We needed to talk about him.

John told me at last what had happened. They had planned to see an exhibition. Alberto did not appear at their usual meeting place. John waited and then decided to go to the exhibition. He hoped Alberto would be there. But Alberto did not turn up. John saw the show, socialized a bit and left.

"I went home hoping to find a message left by Alberto. But no message had been left. Jill had been there all day. There was no sign of Alberto. He was, of course, not reachable by phone. I was feeling apprehensive. Most apprehensive indeed. I woke up to no news. Something had to be wrong. I went to Primrose Mansions and rang his bell. No response. Someone let me into the building. I went up to his front door and rang the bell. No response. I peered through the letter box. Again, no sign of Alberto. All that I managed to see was a crowded corridor. I went to look for the porter. He had not seen Alberto in a few days. I asked him to call the police and keep me fully informed. I thought it best to go home and wait there. The police came. They found Alberto in a coma and took him straight to the hospital. I went to see him there as soon as they gave me access. He was just the way you saw him. I sat with him, read him a bit from a book, I talked to him. Just like you did. Poor Alberto."

Flashes of Alberto's life kept coming to us both. An often difficult but extraordinary life. A poem of his came to mind.

Love

In spite of all there is a love affair
Between me and life

13

It was a most pleasant morning. Alberto would have loved the light, the blue sky. Not the location, though. Not the café. It was a well-known meeting place, full of literary references. Elias Canetti had held court there for many years. It was supposedly there that Brodsky received the news of his own Nobel Prize. It was a place frequented by local poets and writers. But not Alberto. Not him. He actively disliked Hampstead. He only ventured out there to visit his special friends. Paula Rego and Victor Willing and not really many more. I was flattered to be among those chosen few. I often tried to remind him that many artists and writers whom he held in admiration had lived in Hampstead. I tried listing some of them: Constable, Keats, Tagore, Katherine Mansfield, Ben Nicholson, Jacqueline du Pré, Dennis Brain, and so many, many others, including his dear friend Edith Sitwell. Alberto's response was prompt:

"Yes, I know, I visited her there once or twice. But Edith was only there near the end and she never really liked it. She didn't, and neither do I."

But in spite of protestations that Hampstead was "unimaginably far," that the only tube connection was the "dreadful Northern Line" and that, on top of it all, "it attracted tedious groups of nature lovers taking day trips to the Heath," one other justification brought him there: Kenwood House. Alberto went there to contemplate Vermeer's *Girl Playing the Guitar*, and "the best of all self-portraits by Rembrandt, the one in front of a circle." And he quoted Kenneth Clark: "Rembrandt's self-portraits are the greatest autobiography ever presented to posterity."

Alberto met Kenneth Clark in the mid-50s. He held him in high regard and presented him with a copy of his *77 Poems*. In a letter to Alberto, Kenneth Clark had this to say:

"Your lyrics do seem to me to ring with the true music of inspiration, and I have been thrilled to discover a poet who is new to me."

We were lost in reminiscence, John and I. And suddenly John exclaimed:

"Alberto needs an obituary. We should each write one. What do you think? I think we owe it to him."

I could not but agree. Reassuringly, John added:

"I will see to that."

He also offered to deal with other things that needed urgent attention: a death certificate and the funeral arrangements. I took his generous offer with relief and gratitude. I would simply not know how to proceed. The state of Alberto's flat was one of my great concerns. There would be a mess to clear. That much I knew and had seen. But according to Alberto, "things had become a lot worse." I was also preoccupied with money matters. I knew about unpaid bills, credit cards, his overdraft. I had to locate his will. His wishes had to be followed.

I went home to make phone calls. I had not yet talked to Mary. I had gone straight to see John. Mary had to be informed. Alberto's family and friends needed to know what had happened.

The media needed to be notified. And I wanted to find out once and for all if that vanishing key had been located. It was now sadly needed.

14

Mary had expected the worst. But even so, disbelief showed in her voice. The thought of Alberto's death was inconceivable. I gave her a list of people to contact, told her that I would call her back, and proceeded to make some telephone calls myself. Then Mary called from Cascais. She had a few things to tell me. One of the calls that she took had been from former President Mário Soares. He was Alberto's admirer and produced an immediate public statement. It attracted attention right away and people were calling to know. Meanwhile, Alberto's little key had not been found. I told Mary to stop worrying. I had to inform the bank, in any case. She wished me luck. I missed her.

For most of his life in London, Alberto used Barclays Bank. I went to the nearest branch and indicated my need to talk to a desk attendant. A pair of bright blue eyes beckoned me. They belonged to a pale, dark-haired, buxom woman in her forties. She looked jolly and convivial. The name tag on her desk displayed what seemed to be an Irish name. So much the better, I thought. I approached her desk with a smile. She smiled right back at me.

"Good morning. Lovely morning. Can I help you?" Definitely Irish.

"I have an unusual matter to discuss." She looked intrigued for a moment.

"Go on, then!" she said reassuringly.

"Could you please be so kind as to access this account?"

I had Alberto's details in my notebook. I had recently made a money transfer from his stagnant bank account somewhere in Lisbon. All his details were correct.

"Is this your account, sir? Can I see your Barclaycard?"

"As it happens I do bank with you, with Barclays, but this is not my account. It belongs to a friend."

She frowned a little. Her eyes seemed to display a different shade of blue.

"I'm very sorry, sir, but I am not at liberty to access this account at your request."

"I feared as much," I said, "but sadly, my friend is dead. He is not even buried yet. He wanted me to take care of his affairs."

She interrupted me with a gentle moan of sympathy.

"Oh dear! I am so sorry!"

Her eyes were sky blue again.

"You see, my friend was a poet."

I was going to say writer, but I thought that her Irish soul would respond better to poet. Her eyes said yes. And she asked:

"Oh! Was he? I'm so sorry." I proceeded.

"He was a wonderful poet. And a very private person. But in order to take care of his affairs, I need to see his will, that's the first thing. And quite apart from his writings, there will be money matters to sort out. He was always short of money, never had any to keep. I am sure that he had an overdraft and a few outstanding bills. Can you access his account and just tell me if it's true?"

"Let's have a look, then."

She went click, click, click on her keyboard, rested her chin on her hand and said:

"Oh dear! Yes, I can see. Yes, he has actually. Oh dear! Poor thing... was he married?"

I thought it neither opportune nor necessary to discuss any aspect of Alberto's private life.

"No," I said, "he lived alone."

"Sad, isn't it? Poor thing. Was he old?"

"No, not terribly, no." She went click, click, click.

"I cannot show you the screen, you understand, but there are accounts to settle."

"Outstanding bills? Direct debits?"

That was not an idle question. Alberto had things in storage. I had insisted with him to put his storage bill on direct debit. But Alberto always replied that everything was just fine and changed the subject. I asked the Irish lady:

"Could you tell me if there is a recent payment to a warehouse?

"A warehouse? What would he want it for? This is a bit of a story, isn't it?" New shades of blue in her eyes. And she went on:

"Well, I wouldn't be able to give you the details, of course, but actually, no… I don't see any payment to anything like that."

I was beginning to feel that my questions could be perceived as suspicious.

"Just one more thing," I said. "As I was saying to you, the most important thing seems to be to find his will. He has it in a safe-deposit box with Barclays Bank. He actually sent me a key. But I don't have it with me. I don't live in London, you see? I live abroad and took a plane straight away without bringing that key. And what's more, he told me where his box was kept but I can't remember where. What do you think I can do? And where can that box be kept?"

"This is a Sloane Square account. An old one, I can see. The safe-deposit box may well be kept in the Strand. But I would go to Sloane Square and ask them there. They will know. Shall I give you the address?"

"No thank you, I know it well."

"Oh good," she said.

I stood up and she stood up. She tilted forward a little. I half expected a hug.

"Thank you so much for your help."

"That's all right, love, I'm so sorry. So sorry for your lonely poet friend! What a shame! And all the best. Good luck, dear. God bless!"

I shook hands with her and set off on my way to Sloane Square.

My sense of loss had returned. A rush of fast moving images filled my mind. The last one, the still, frail, small body in the hospital, kept returning. All the way down to Sloane Square I struggled with the urge to weep. And suddenly, there it was, Sloane Square. The Royal Court Theatre at one end, Peter Jones across the way, Sloane Street to the side, King's Road flowing from the square. I was in Alberto's kingdom. These were Alberto's streets. He crossed them both in ecstasy and in pain. He walked along them with expectations, dreams, hopes, dashed hopes, poems on his mind, soliloquies. He wrote poems in these streets. Poems of distilled emotion that speak of being there. To one of those I return time and again.

Sequence

The singing of the birds in Margaretta Terrace
A slightly cool April evening
Memories of the time when I walked aflame past Oakley Street
(A certain window)
Everything overlaid confused unresolved
Death (including the death of sentiments) is a facile word that
      does not fit
Unresolved
Everything overlaid confused unresolved
    I carry on walking home Phené Street Oakley Gardens
        Chelsea Manor Street St. Loo Avenue Flood Street
            Royal Hospital Road   52 Tite Street

For more than twenty years Alberto lived in rented rooms. His favourite and longest lasting lodgings were at 52 Tite Street. His hosts were Mrs Hope-Nicholson and her son Felix. More House, as it was called, was a large Victorian mansion built in 1882. Besides its architectural interest, it contained a treasure trove of *objets d'art* and antiques. Manuel Bandeira, the Brazilian modernist poet who visited Alberto there, wrote a chronicle describing its

With Jacqueline & Felix Hope-Nicholson, Tite Street, London.

extraordinary contents. He added that Alberto had chosen to live there, preferring eccentricity over comfort. The house was originally the home of the Nicholson family. Jacqueline Hope-Nicholson and her former husband Hedley, were both well-known eccentrics. Alberto never knew them as a couple. They were genealogists and lovers of all the arts. Jacqueline was also a heraldic specialist and pageantry costume designer. Hedley, a Charles I devotee, was the founder of the Society of King Charles the Martyr. The house chapel contained a fragment of the tunic that Charles I wore at his execution. Among various other books, Hedley Hope-Nicholson wrote the memorably titled *The Mindes Delight or: A Variety of Memorable Matters Worthy of Observation*.

Tite Street itself was worthy of observation. Oscar Wilde, John Singer Sargent, Whistler and Augustus John had lived there at different times. Alberto was one of the guests at the

unveiling of the plaque placed on Oscar Wilde's house. The ceremony was attended by a galaxy of cultural figures. One of the speakers was Sir Compton McKenzie. Augustus John, T.S. Eliot, John Hayward, Sacheverell Sitwell, Michael Redgrave and Rachel Kempson, as well as Oscar Wilde's own son, Vyvyan Holland, were there. Alberto was there. He belonged. He lived in Chelsea. Life was often hard but heady. He was young and he felt free.

With Manuel Bandeira, Trafalgar Square, London, 1957.

The Sloane Square branch of Barclays Bank was almost unrecognisable. The old counter had disappeared and given way to a sleek, very business-like environment. I knew that branch very well. I had used it in the past.

Alberto's relationship with Barclays Bank was best described as conflictual. His way of life, his manner, his irregular income, his proudly shown incapacity to deal with money matters, collided with the guidelines of standard banking procedures. Sticking to his guns Alberto insisted that banks should keep a Robin Hood attitude towards their regular clients: make money from those who had it and lend it to those who needed it. The problem was that in contrast with his insufficient funds, Alberto's patterns of spending left a trail of what was seen as sheer extravagance. Payments made to West End galleries, theatre agencies, bookshops, could not be met by small cheques issued in weak foreign currencies by such unknown institutions as *Jornal do Brasil, O Século* and *Rádio Clube de Moçambique*. The odd BBC cheque restored some credibility to his erratic income. Bank managers denied credit. Alberto became indignant and called them philistines. Rows and humiliations followed. He got deeper and deeper into debt. "A torment" he used to say. And recalling a complaint that he heard from Edith Sitwell, he went into further detail: "Money eats the blood." Quoting it brought no relief, but it gave a higher status to his permanent affliction.

The bank attendant I saw was no blue eyed Irish lady. He was a balding young man wearing a tight suit and rimless glasses. His eyes darted everywhere, keeping track of everything. A rather unsettling trait. I greeted him, gave him Alberto's details and went straight to the point.

"Can you please check this account? It belongs to a long-standing customer of yours. He always came to this branch. I am very sorry to tell you that he died. He was a writer. I am his literary executor. This gentleman kept his will in a safe-deposit box. Do you keep it here, by any chance?"

He did not say anything. He checked Alberto's details, looked at his screen and replied:

"Yes, I know. I know the gentleman." He was clearly not a talker.

"He died!" I repeated dryly.

"I'm sorry to hear it."

"Is his safe-deposit box kept here? Can you tell me?"

He did not answer for a little while. He was looking at the screen. He did not go click, click, click, like the nice Irish lady. His fingers moved very fast and lightly on the keyboard. He did not look particularly interested in either Alberto or me. I wondered if he really knew Alberto. I doubted it very strongly. I noticed that he wore a golden bracelet on his wrist.

"Well?" I asked with impatience.

"No boxes here, sir. Try the West End. St James's or Regent Street. Try the Strand. Anything else?"

"No. Good bye."

I took the metro again to Piccadilly. I had to find the branch that kept the box. Would they let me look inside it? How could that little key have disappeared? I tried to persuade myself that having lost it was not an ominous sign. But as those thoughts kept pursuing me, I kept hearing Alberto's voice asking me, time and again, to take care of his writings after he died. He always apologized for the "macabre conversation" and what he called "the dreadful task" of dealing with all his papers and also of making sure that a few things that he owned would be passed on as gifts.

"I am so sorry, but you see? Who can I ask? Of all my surviving friends no one knows me like you do. I know it's an imposition. But who can make head or tail of certain things that I say? All my references are lost from place to place. And there is a trail of people and countries where I have lived and even jobs that I took that I share with no one else. And besides... there is the language!"

He meant the Portuguese language that inspired him to write a celebrated poem.

The Portuguese Language

> This language that I love
> With its barbarous cut
> Its honey
> Its hellenic salt
> And olive
> This limpidity
> Which so often
> Has a deaf halo
> This wonder
> So massacred
> By nearly all who speak it
> This languor

This singing
Amphora
This manly sword
So graceful
Capable of brandishing all the ways
Of all the airs
Of all the dances
This voice
This superb
Language
Capable of all the colours
Of all the risks
Of expression
(And wins always the game)
Capable of everything
Like a woman really
In love
This language
Is my constant India
My endless wedding
My love for ever
My dissipation
My eternal
Virginity

19

I talked to a few bank employees. They varied in manner, voice and way of dressing. I chose to start at St. James's and was referred to the Strand. Just as the blue eyed Irish lady had originally said. The Strand.

This, once again, was Alberto's territory. And mine. For both of us the Strand started on the steps of the National Gallery, and continued all the way to the entrance of Bush House. It looked quite different now. I missed my old landmarks. There was a splendid book dealer where I found a first edition of Gertrude Stein's *Tender Buttons*. The price was beyond my limit. I told Alberto all about it. He chided me for my timidity.

"You simply have to take risks. That sort of thing disappears. One has to make sacrifices." Vintage Alberto advice. Now,

With Ruben García, Trafalgar Square, London, 1970s.

that book dealer was gone. A piano shop next to it, prodigal in trills and arpeggios that softened the traffic noise, was also gone. Pleasant pubs, collector shops, a tobacconist, were gone. Sandwich shops, fast food restaurants, chain coffee houses, mobile and clothes outlets were everywhere. They were strangely out of place. I kept walking. St. Mary le Strand was in sight. I thought of countless visits to the Courtauld Institute, with Alberto. He enjoyed looking at specific paintings in the Gallery, and, as he put it, "having a drink with Manet at the *Bar des Folies-Bergère*," and also "saying hello to the Bloomsbury artists."

"They are unequal, I know, but they have a special charm. And quite frankly, England owes them the enjoyment of modern painting. To Roger Fry, above all."

King's College. Alberto and I met Pablo Neruda at an event held at King's. A reception and a reading. Neruda's wife shared Alberto's family name. Neruda brought him over to a group where she was chatting so that she could meet a relative who was a Portuguese poet. A glass of Chilean wine was raised by Pablo Neruda to all the poets of Portugal. And there, on my own, years later, I was delighted to meet Octavio Paz. He was a friend of Alberto's. He published Alberto's poems in his magazine, *Vuelta*, and translated them as well.

I could not really remember having seen a Barclays branch anywhere along the Strand. But fragments of the past kept coming back. London seemed to be determined to keep Alberto alive. And suddenly there it was, Barclays Bank. Yes, of course, there it was. I walked in. More bank officials. I told my story again.

"Yes, we do keep safe-deposit boxes. If you can wait just a bit, I will check our records to see if we have the box you want."

I waited for quite a while. Young people came in and out. Probably King's College students. Maybe people from Bush House. Both Alberto and I had worked there. Bush House was the headquarters of the BBC world service. Alberto was brought to London with a BBC contract. His contract was not renewed. They gave him some freelance work. He became what was described as an outside contributor. Alberto commented on the meaning of outside. Outside. Not in. He was an excellent broadcaster.

More people walked in and out. Tellers started to return from their lunch break. People used the cash machines. I was waiting. And then a voice called for me from a desk right at the end. A young man in shirt sleeves signalled to me.

"Good afternoon!" I said.

He said "Hi." I found it strange. His jacket was draped around the back of his chair. The chair had wheels. He rolled the chair to and fro. He wore a bright orange tie.

"We do have that client's box," he announced.

"Oh, good!"

"Yes, but the point is this. Do you have any credential that will permit you to open it and verify its contents? And do you have with you a death certificate to prove that our client is dead?"

"Not yet. That aspect is being dealt with right now. But the credential you want is surely inside the box. I mean, his will, of course."

With Octavio Paz, Cambridge, MA, 1972.

"The box belongs to the client. We can only let you have it with our client's permission."

"But he's dead. My friend is dead. His will is inside the box that you keep on his behalf."

"The bank has to follow rules. First of all you have to prove that our client is dead. Officially dead, I mean. Then you have to give us proof that you have our client's consent to have access to the box. And that is the only way."

I could not quarrel with that. But I disliked the young man. I disliked his voice, his manner, his jacket dangling askew from the back of his chair, his rolling chair, his horrendous orange tie. No Irish lady, here. I thought Alberto would have liked her. Once in a blue moon he came from a bank experience saying: "Can you imagine? What luck! It seems that I've been adopted by the current bank manager. How unusually wonderful."

The thought of obtaining a credential to open Alberto's box was bothering me. What kind of a credential? And who could possibly issue it? Then a thought came to my mind. The Embassy of Portugal, of course. After all, I had retired from there not long ago. London was my final posting. They knew me well at the Embassy. I found a telephone box and dialed the old number. A very familiar voice answered my call. After a friendly exchange I asked to be put through to the Ambassador's office.

"I'm afraid that he's not in," said the receptionist. "But if you give me a moment I will put you through to our new Chargé d'Affaires."

As luck would have it, the new Chargé d'Affaires had worked with me in the past. He took my call right away.

"Well... What a wonderful surprise! What brought you here to London? My goodness, what a surprise. And how long will you be staying? My goodness. What a surprise!"

I explained all that had happened and asked him if he could help.

"Of course, of course, a credential... Have you met the new Ambassador?" Yes, I had, but just in passing, somewhere in the Foreign Ministry.

"Oh good!... That's good. And tell me... what kind of a credential do you need? I'm sure that the Ambassador will instruct someone to issue it... Absolutely. I am sure. I am quite sure of that. The trouble is, he is not here. I mean, not here right now. He's expected back quite soon but... this is quite a coincidence, so is our Foreign Minister. The Ambassador will be with him, naturally, and that means that everything will be my responsibility. I will do whatever you need as soon as the Ambassador tells me how he wants me to proceed. So this is the situation... I'm sorry, tell me again, what did you say the poet's name was? Oh! I see!... My condolences, I'm so sorry."

I suggested that the Consulate could perhaps come to my rescue.

"Ah! Well… that is an idea. That's a very good idea, but there is a problem there, a different one, as it happens. Our London-based community has grown so terribly much! The Consulate is overwhelmed. Amazing! It's quite amazing. And you would have to meet in person with the Consul General, of course. He's new. He is also new. Another curious coincidence… The trouble is that he tends to be difficult to find, that is the problem. Oh my goodness, the Ambassador will be here very shortly! I'm afraid I have to go. But do come by, don't forget. We are expecting your visit. We really are. So nice to hear your voice. And, of course, count on us…"

"Yes! Of course. Good to hear your voice again. Bye!"

I called Mary in the evening. The press in Lisbon had already reported Alberto's death. Mary told me that a journalist from the Portuguese news agency had phoned expecting to have an informal chat with me about Alberto. I made a note of his name to call him back. But I did it with a touch of apprehension. I recognized in that call an opportunity to reach beyond the strictly literary public. But I also felt the need to protect Alberto's name. Having lived his life abroad he was vulnerable to conjecture. I feared some wrong allusions and, perhaps worse, wrong conclusions about his life and "career." Alberto had always rejected the mere thought of a career. He treasured his anonymity. He was above all a poet. He claimed that anonymity kept him free to frequent his inner world and to consort with the muses. I was feeling sad and anxious. I missed Mary. It was August. At that time, in Cascais, Mary and I took gentle walks to the sea.

John rang me to let me know that Alberto's death certificate would be ready for collection. I brought him up to date on my endeavours and suggested that he met me at the bank bringing a copy of the much needed certificate. I thought that having John there as a witness would improve my credibility. We agreed to meet at Barclays at midday. I made it down to the Strand with time to spare and felt a strong compulsion to walk to Waterloo Bridge.

I watched the flow of the river, the barges, St Paul's beautiful dome the other way, and looking ahead of me, Hungerford Bridge, the profile of the Houses of Parliament, and the effect of the light on the surface of the water. I was lost in contemplation and the memory of so many works of art that those views have inspired. The river was slow that morning.

Alberto too loved that bridge. He crossed it almost daily. He was a regular visitor of the whole South Bank complex and he enjoyed meeting his friends at the Riverside Café. He had a favourite table where he wrote, consulted performance calendars and planned his ticket purchases. There was a ledge by his side where he kept all his belongings. From where he sat he could contemplate the Thames. He ranted with indignation at the renovation work that "ruined and disfigured" one of his favourite spots. Later, he found another table at the upstairs bar of the main building. That table was preferred as an evening meeting point. For Alberto, crossing the Waterloo Bridge was an event in itself. It brought him memories, reveries. Poems happened.

Ecstasy

The-afternoon-glides-white-boat
Sudden pavanne

The heart stops

The sun waits

Liquid shores

Time dances very slowly

22

John and I met at the bank. John brought with him extra copies of Alberto's death certificate. It indicated quite clearly that the informant was John. It was right there, very clearly – *Informant: John McEwen.* I felt more confident. Two young women came towards us. I described the situation once again. They seemed aware of it. They thanked us for producing Alberto's death certificate but continued to insist that a credential was needed. The same old story again. I proceeded to explain that it was important to enter Alberto's flat knowing what he wanted done with what was there. One of them replied politely:

"Sir, access to our client's private address is an entirely different matter. The bank has no responsibility in that area."

"I know," I said, "Yes, I know. Of course. But this has to be resolved. Look. Mr de Lacerda was a Portuguese citizen. So am I. Until my recent retirement I held a diplomatic post at our

With Fernando Alves, in Alberto's restaurant, 2005.

Embassy here. Would it help if an Embassy official came here to vouch for me?"

I was trying to be persuasive without apparent success. The other young woman said: "Not really!..."

I tried another alternative:

"Would you possibly consider opening that box in front of a police officer?" The two looked at each other. The first one took her turn. She said:

"Not really!..."

But I went on. I felt encouraged by John's distinguished presence by my side:

"You see... that flat is full of writings and other items of interest. Items of interest to Portugal and Britain and other nations, France, the US, Brazil, Spain. What is there is part of history. Cultural history, I mean. Your client, Mr Alberto de Lacerda, needs your protection of course. But the poet, Alberto de Lacerda, whose literary estate I am supposed to look after, needs my own. I have to honour his wishes. Please understand that I need to gain access to the box that you are keeping."

The young women's responses seemed to be pendular. We were back with the other one. She asked me: "Are you sure that your name will be mentioned in the contents of the box?"

Both John and I said "Yes!" at the same time.

They took a couple of steps back and conferred with one another. I wondered which one of them would now be the first to speak. I made a mental guess. I failed. The last one spoke again.

"This is all a bit irregular, but we will look inside the box. We will see if your name is mentioned. Could you give us a valid proof of identity, please?... Do you have your passport with you?"

I handed it over promptly.

"Thank you... but you have to be informed that we are not in a position to open any sealed document. We will talk to our manager, now... Let us see what he decides!"

They went away for what seemed to be a long time. They came back with a grey metal box. One of them held it and the other opened it. By then I did not care who was who and in what order. The one who had a free hand gave me my passport back and also a white envelope.

"It was not sealed, sir," she said. "And indeed, your name is mentioned." They both smiled. I thanked them both.

I picked up the envelope and made a gesture to open it.

"No," said John. "Let us wait. Let us open it at lunch. Let us go to Alberto's restaurant." Alberto's envelope was in my pocket. We walked to Alberto's restaurant. Its location was across the river. Waterloo Road. Under the span of the bridge.

23

Alberto discovered that restaurant after a concert at the Festival Hall. The manager and the staff were Portuguese. Alberto heard them speak the language. Unusually, as he tended to avoid what he called "national celebrations abroad," he addressed them all in Portuguese. They were delighted to serve him and Alberto enjoyed the atmosphere, the food and the blessing of no music. He was touched by the staff's attentiveness and discretion and from that moment on, "the restaurant under the bridge" became Alberto's restaurant. He brought all of his friends there. Both John and I knew it well.

We sat at Alberto's table, ordered lunch and a bottle of wine. We filled our glasses and raised them in Alberto's memory.

"To the immortal memory!" said John.

I felt that I should say something in Portuguese. I had a lump in my throat. I could only say his name.

"Alberto."

We each took a sip of wine. Then John said:

"I think that now is the moment to open the envelope." I did. It said:

> I give, devise and bequeath the whole of my estate, both real and personal, of whatsoever kind and wherever situated to Luís Amorim de Sousa. I appoint the same Luís Amorim de Sousa my sole executor.

I was instantly overcome with deep emotion and a near sense of panic. In every sense of the word Alberto's will was too much. We drank to Alberto again. I checked the date of the will. Alberto had kept it a secret for nearly twenty years. Mr Antunes, the manager, came up to greet us. We told him the sad news. He was clearly shocked. He said:

"Mr Alberto de Lacerda was a very special customer. He came here often alone, but also with distinguished guests. He was very nice to us. A true gentleman he was. He always reserved this table for all his special occasions. He will be greatly missed by us all." And turning to the staff he told them: "We lost Senhor Alberto de Lacerda."

He said it in Portuguese. Then John asked me: "Do you think that we should go to Alberto's flat?"

We hailed a cab just outside the restaurant. John told the driver: "Prince of Wales Drive, please."

With Roman Jakobson, Electra Cardona, Svatava Jakobson and Paul Schmidt, Austin, TX, 1968.

24

I had not been to Alberto's flat in a few years. I remembered very well how full it was. Full and untidy. Since then, Alberto had warned me, things had become a lot worse. On my last visit there I sat on the only bit of sofa that was free from piles of books. There were a few cardboard boxes in the middle of the room. Alberto himself had sent them home from Boston. They appeared to be used as extra tables. More books were piled on them. It was difficult to walk around the room. In the middle of all that, said Alberto, there was a photo archive. I had never heard about it.

"A photo archive?" I asked him. "A proper photo archive?"

"A splendid photo archive," replied Alberto. "Somewhere in here. Or there." He pointed to the bedroom wall, and added:

"I don't really know. Here or there. I will deal with it one day."

I noticed his notebooks. He had some of them scattered around. Hardbound, large size, black covers. He bought them all as he needed them, in the same art supplies shop. In Chelsea, naturally. They contained diary entries and poems. Lots of poems. "Hundreds of unpublished poems," said Alberto. "Maybe one thousand, who knows?" And letters. I also saw piles of letters. He never threw them away. Lots of newspapers, too. He threw away some of those. Not many, not very often. Along the corridor, his shelves were stacked full of LPs. There were objects here and there. Things that he owned. His things. But a few years had gone by. I feared that there would be a lot more to deal with. Alberto had said so. More than once. And not a word to suggest what I should to do with it all. I felt both honoured and humbled by Alberto's trust in me. And overwhelmed at the thought of what to do. The cab turned into Prince of Wales Drive, and there it was: Primrose Mansions. A threshold.

John went to look for the porter. I leaned on the outside wall of that familiar building. Alberto lived there for more than thirty years. His flat had been occupied by colleagues of mine who knew him. As they were vacating it they suggested that Alberto could possibly take it over. I knew the flat. A pleasant two room flat with a good size corridor. I thought it a good idea and told Alberto all about it. He was reluctant at first but agreed to go and see it. The rent was "miraculously low." The only negative point was the location. South of the river. But opposite Battersea Park. That was a plus. And he liked Prince of Wales Drive. The Chelsea Bridge to the right, the Albert Bridge to the left. Those bridges appealed to him. He saw a plaque on a wall for Sean O'Casey. He liked that.

"First, Oscar Wilde then O'Casey," he commented later on. "Theatrical neighbours, always. What comedies, what tragedies, what happenings!"

The flat was the right size. I was immensely relieved when Alberto agreed to take it. A place where he could feel free.

It was hard to realize that thirty years had gone by. Thirty years of a full life. Thirty years gathering things. And now I had to decide what to do with all of them. All of them and a lot more. All that was stored in the warehouse where he kept the overflow of what he could not fit inside the flat. He had told me about that. He rented a storage unit. He never said where it was. I simply knew there was one. A unit in a warehouse. A warehouse somewhere in London. It was all quite overwhelming.

John appeared with the porter. The porter led us both upstairs. He told us his name was Wayne. He unlocked the door and said "It's very messy, I warn you." John and I tried to walk in and pushed the door a bit further. Something seemed to be blocking it. It opened part of the way. We squeezed in. Behind the door there was a huge pile of letters. They covered the whole door frame.

25

The corridor had become a hazardous pathway. There were obstacles and litter. Things crunched under every step. It was very hard to guess what was crunching underfoot. There were newspapers and letters, more letters and more newspapers, and plastic bags everywhere. Some of those had things inside. Wayne told us that Alberto was found lying in the sitting room. It was difficult to see where he had fallen. More difficult to imagine how he had been taken out, presumably on a stretcher. Not a single piece of furniture could be seen. Everything had disappeared under a mountain of books, more newspapers, CDs, empty CD holders, LPs, pictures fallen off the walls, chocolate wrappers, empty packets of Thai crisps, more plastic bags, a lot more cardboard boxes, things piled up on top of things, and topping a leaning pyramid, turned upside down, legs up, a chair that could not find space on the floor. I put my foot on a book. Manuel Bandeira. One of Alberto's favourite poets and also a keen promoter of Alberto's own poetry in Brazil. I stepped on a CD holder. Bill Evans. Alberto loved his music. He had all of his recordings. They met briefly in the States. Alberto had his address written on a paper napkin that he showed me, together with a signed photo.

"I never wrote to Bill Evans. I wrote about him, instead."

On the floor, next to Bill Evans, I found a Robert Creeley biography. Alberto became interested in his poetry after discovering *For Love*. Robert Creeley came to London. Alberto attended a reading and enjoyed the way he read. He particularly enjoyed Creeley's intoning of the word relation/ship. Years later they met in Texas. They got on extremely well. After a party that Alberto gave in Austin, Robert Creeley wrote these words on a copy of another book of his:

For Alberto/ With thanks for the sounds he moves in/ With love/ Bob.

Alberto loved that inscription. The party was in celebration of a large poetry festival held at the University. Robert Duncan described the festival as "an ecstasy of poet's company." Jorge Luis Borges was there. Octavio Paz was there. Louis Zukofsky was there, Czesław Miłosz was there. Alberto was a moving force behind the organization of the festival. He shared a reading session with his old London friend David Wevill and Borges and Robert Duncan. Alberto and Duncan continued to see each other and exchanged letters for years. Alberto visited him and his partner, the artist Jess, in San Francisco. Later, Robert Duncan returned the visit. They saw each other in Boston and in London. Duncan came to Primrose Mansions.

Up on a shelf, now, I spotted a Duncan book. I could not reach it to read Duncan's inscription. I knew that there would be one. There were lots of poetry books on the shelves. And art books. And books about music and biography. Alberto's world. Peeking from under a heap of crumpled paper I noticed a small golden frame. I rescued it. It contained a watercolour. A sky view.

With Jorge Luis Borges and Robert Duncan,
International Poetry Festival, Austin, TX, 1969.

A stern landscape. Clouds rolling over grey hills. A landscape full of air. Air that you could almost breathe. Bracing air. The artist was a pre-Victorian. Charles William Day. I had never heard his name. I looked for a safe spot to place the little picture. It was difficult to find one there in the middle of that disheartening spectacle. Neglect. Heartbreaking loneliness. I could hear John in the kitchen. He ran taps and cleared the fridge of things that had gone bad.

Wayne, the porter, could not cope. He left us amid the chaos. I ventured into the bedroom. It was deplorable. Alberto's bed was a sight. Dishevelled would not describe it. It was surrounded by letters. A lot of them were unopened. There were books, always more books. Also a few scattered clothes. Worn out clothes. And poems. Loose poems by Alberto's bedside. I gathered them with respect. The dead telephone was there. A silent witness to Alberto's lonely life.

There were pictures on the wall. Most of them hung crookedly. I found great visual relief with the discovery of a graceful painting, a magnolia, by an unknown artist. A white magnolia in a glass of water on a light blue flat surface. The contours of the flower, tilting sweetly to one side, reminded me of a ballerina on stage. I could not get close enough to see who might have painted it. A much later discovery revealed two entwined initials FR. The artist was Frances Richards. Alberto's parka, a present from Paula Rego, lay abandoned on the bed. I noticed a small address book. I picked it up right away hoping that it would enable me to get in touch with his friends.

I did not know how long we had been in the flat. John called from the bathroom door. An old shirt on a hanger was dangling over the bath. A poignant image. Heartbreaking. And John said:

"We should go now. It's enough. We need to get out of here. Let us go. Poor Alberto!" We were both extremely shaken.

26

As we were leaving the flat I noticed a brown envelope on the floor. Some strange impulse made me look at it. I did. The sender was a warehouse. I could not read the date on the post mark. I pocketed it and followed John out of the building. We were in the street again. There was air and there was space and there was light. Alberto kept his heavy curtains permanently drawn at home. He did it to protect his pictures from the sun. He loved the light. Natural light. But not if it shone on his pictures. He claimed that the purifying effects of the light cleaned everything. In what concerned works of art he made the point of explaining that purifying meant wiping out. And he wanted all his pictures to remain in mint condition. No natural light ever came into his flat. Out in the open I never saw Alberto in sunglasses. I never saw him shield his eyes from the sun. He celebrated light throughout his life.

> Water
> My first element
>
> Fire
> Later
>
> Light
>
> Light is now
> My slow element
> For ever

John hailed a cab once again. "Let's have a drink at the Chelsea Arts Club!"

Alberto had mentioned it often but I had never been there. A drink would be most welcome. And I was curious about the Chelsea Arts Club. It was extremely hard to get over the shock of what we had just seen. All that appalling disorder, the overwhelming sadness of that once romantic flat, its crushing solitude. The taxi was now crossing Chelsea Bridge. And then, I opened the brown envelope from the warehouse. The letter that it contained warned Alberto that his bill was long outstanding and indicated a final date for its settlement. After that date, the items kept there in storage would be removed and disposed of. That final date was overdue by one day. I showed the letter to John. We were both seized by the same instant panic. There was a dreadful precedent to that letter.

Many years earlier, one morning, Alberto called me at home. It was a Saturday morning.

"Do you think that you can meet me in town? I would be most grateful if you could." He sounded preoccupied.

"Do you mean now?"

"Please. I would really appreciate it if you could."

I sensed a crisis and went. As soon as I met Alberto he stopped a taxi. I did not know where we were going. The taxi stopped outside a large warehouse. Alberto had kept very unusually silent all the way. He handed me some sort of ticket and said:

"Can you please be so kind as to go in there and ask about my things? I don't want to go in. I will wait here in the car."

I went in, holding that ticket. A young man came towards me. He was extremely affable.

"Good morning. Can I help you?"

He smiled broadly and took my bit of paper. He looked at it, always smiling, nodded and said:

"Oh, yes. I know. Unfortunately the contents of this unit have been disposed of. The bill was long overdue. Are you the client?"

"No, I'm not. I am enquiring on his behalf."

"Sorry. We did warn the gentleman, we did. We warned him a few times. Let me just check once again... Yeah! This unit was cleared a few days ago. Sorry! I'm really sorry. But I think... give me a minute... I think we have something there..."

He walked into a side room and came back carrying a box. Some sort of archive box.

"There you are. He can have this. These things were kept. I'll let you have them. So sorry!" He smiled throughout all of this. I took the box to Alberto. He knew right away what had happened. He folded his left arm around his middle, hid his face with his free hand and cried. He sobbed like a child. I simply did not know what to do. I just sat next to him. The cab driver saw it all and said very gently:

"Where to, now?"

Alberto composed himself and said: "The West End. Anywhere in the West End."

Then he turned to me, his face looked so very sad, and he exclaimed: "I have lost my whole life. All my souvenirs are gone." Then he was silent again. It was a very sad day.

With Scott Laughlin, Washington, DC, 1994.

27

Now, once again in a cab, I feared the repetition of that loss. I had the mobile with me. I picked up the threatening letter and called the warehouse. John was looking straight at me. A young man's voice took the call. I gave him Alberto's client number and the details of the letter.

"I'm sorry sir, I'm only minding the phone. The manager is in a meeting. I can't reach him right now."

"You've got to. Please listen. This is really most important. You see, this client has died. That is why he did not pay. What I am trying to do is to protect the contents of his unit. I am talking about items of international interest. Please let me talk to the manager."

"I know nothing about it, sir. I'm only minding the phone."

"Yes, I know. You told me that. But I really must insist, can I please talk to the manager? Can you please let him know that I need to talk to him? This is really important."

John, sitting there by my side, was showing signs of anxiety. We were both extremely anxious. The boy sounded quite unfazed.

"I'm only following orders. I'm new here." I snapped at him:

"Time to learn that there are things that need immediate attention. Please call the manager." Silence.

"Will you please call the manager?"

The boy responded with a muted exclamation. I think that he said "fuck!" There was a pause. A long one. Then he said: "I'll tell him when he comes out. You'd better leave me your contact number, then." I gave him the number, thanked him and felt that trying to save Alberto's world from destruction was going to be an odyssey. So did John. He asked me: "Do you know what he kept in that unit?"

"Essentially, the contents of his American flat."

"Good heavens!" said John.

When he retired from Boston University Alberto had to vacate his flat. It was completely full. With the generous help of students, he gathered empty cardboard boxes from local stores and packed them up as he could. It was an exhausting task that filled him with angst and nostalgia. They were all randomly packed. Some of them were now piled up in Primrose Mansions. They were the wreckage of the Boston tidal wave.

"Were there any pictures there?" asked John.

"Yes, most probably. But which ones?"

Every time he taught a new semester in the States, Alberto brought pictures from London. Then he brought them back again, replaced them with different ones, and to these he added others because, as he once explained: "these images keep me company."

Our taxi left us at the Chelsea Arts Club. As soon as I walked in I saw why Alberto liked it.

28

The whole atmosphere of the Club was very Alberto-like. The mixture of bohemia and eccentricity was suggestively reminiscent of the same cultural circles that welcomed him to London. Alberto was then very young. He was 23 years old. A BBC interview with Roy Campbell led to an introduction to Edith Sitwell. Their friendship flourished immediately. The young exotic Portuguese poet, born in the Governor's palace of the Island of Mozambique, Prospero's island, as it has been called, was now a member of the Sitwells' circle. Alberto's café lifestyle in Lisbon moved to the Sesame Club. There, Edith Sitwell introduced him to the best of London. Among many other stories, he delighted in reporting that he once had tea with Dylan Thomas. And typically, he added: "Tea! With Dylan Thomas! A rare occasion, no doubt. Can you imagine?"

Alberto soon became more than Edith Sitwell's guest. He was her escort, her confidant, her close friend. She dedicated some poems and an entire book to him. That book, a Swinburne anthology, carries the following dedication:

This anthology / is dedicated by the compiler to / ALBERTO DE LACERDA / who suggested the making of it / E.S.

Once inside the Chelsea Arts Club, John ordered two glasses of wine and suggested that we took them to the garden. We sat inside a peaceful gazebo. It had been a very difficult day. It was hard to reconcile Alberto's death with all that had been happening since then. We were both falling silent and talking at the same time. And then my mobile rang. It was the manager of Alberto's warehouse.

"I understand you wanted to have a word with me," he said.

"Thank you so much for returning my call. And please, do thank your assistant. I really appreciate it. I was so very insistent because I am worried about the unit rented by Mr Alberto de Lacerda. Your assistant may have told you that he died. I am his executor. I have just been to his flat. That is where I found the letter that you sent him. I realize that his bill is overdue. I will deal with everything. But you see, I live abroad. I have a lot to sort out. What I really want to ask you is to give me enough time to resolve this situation."

"I don't know that I can. We are in the process of recovering his unit and disposing of its contents!"

"This is exactly why I am appealing to you. Mr Alberto de Lacerda was an internationally known poet and his estate is of literary importance in various countries, including the United Kingdom! Please believe me!"

The manager's response left me more anxious than ever. He said:

"The men have already been."

My heart sank at these words. And he continued: "That unit contained more than two hundred boxes. This bill has been outstanding for longer than we usually tolerate. We are within our legal rights to recover our unit."

I hoped that my appeal did not sound like a whimper. I wanted to sound authoritative.

"I am quite aware of that. But Mr Alberto de Lacerda's estate cannot be lost. That simply cannot happen. His work ranks with the best. Please stop those men. Please do!"

The manager's response was dry.

"I will call you back in a few minutes."

John and I must have gulped our drinks. The tension was unbelievable. And then the phone rang once more. It was the manager.

"I have known that gentleman for years. I'm sorry he died. But he was a difficult customer, you know. Anyway, we are in luck. The men were there but did not take anything. They were there to check the volume of the contents of the unit. I will give you a couple of days. But that bill must be settled."

I was about to say thank you but he said, "I checked the gentleman on the internet. I gathered that he must have been someone. I had no idea. Anyway if you come by tomorrow, we will deal with the paperwork. But that bill must be paid."

29

A great weight was lifted. John and I were leaving our gazebo at the Chelsea Arts Club in a buoyant mood. And then my phone rang again. We were going past some tables. It was my daughter, Sophia. I was telling her the great news. Possibly a bit too vivaciously. Having succeeded in stopping the second catastrophic destruction of Alberto's treasured belongings, I may well have been enthusiastic enough to attract some attention from Club members. I felt that I was being noticed. An employee rushed towards me. He looked flustered. I was transgressing a rule.

"Excuse me sir. You will have to terminate your conversation. Mobile phones are not allowed in the Chelsea Arts Club."

My first message from Alberto somewhere in the great beyond reached me with ballistic power: he was applauding. Not me. Not the rescue of his things. He was applauding the Chelsea Arts Club's directive. Strictly no mobile phones.

Alberto's flat had to be properly seen. I went back to Primrose Mansions with João. The shock persisted. If anything, it increased. Following the terrible impact of my first visit there, I was now faced with the task of dealing with all that chaos. Rather absurdly, I thought of T.S. Eliot's line from 'The Waste Land', *mixing memory and desire*, and gave it an entirely different meaning. Haunted by Alberto's memory I now felt a strong desire to bring him out of obscurity. The extremely sad obscurity of his last few years. Alberto's trust in me was my mandate. I wanted to celebrate the quality of his life, his creative work, his taste, his friendships and significant encounters, his cosmopolitan nature, his lively curiosity.

Alberto was not a stage-seeker. He loved proximity but treasured his anonymity. He loved conviviality but needed his solitude. He loved the buzz of great cities but called silence his master. He brought attention to others but hated to be promoted. He cultivated the pleasures and the rewards of discovery and that was his own preferred way of being reached by his readers. And he also loved to share the things he loved. The promise I made myself was to share his world with others.

João did not know Alberto's flat. After some inescapable exclamations he looked at me and asked:

"Where shall we start?"

Having said this he embarked on a reconnaissance tour, trying not to step on things, a lot of them hardly visible. He picked up obvious rubbish and tried to put it aside. But that, he quickly discovered, was a problematic task. There was rubbish and disorder. They were in a tight embrace. Discarded bags contained things. I had noticed that before. Quite a number of them did. Together with old receipts and coupons and newspapers, those awful discarded bags could also be hiding treasures, souvenirs, things to be salvaged. This turned out to be the case. Interesting things appeared.

I was in the sitting room. Alberto had entertained there with great pleasure. He was visited by friends who were thrilled to be surrounded by his choice of pictures, books, unusual objects. A lovely "studiolo." That is how he thought of it: his "studiolo." His ability to create visual surprise was a feature of his sense of décor. He knew the steps from surprise to enchantment, from stillness to serenity. He also raged. He knew pain. He fought many-headed dragons. But for him, his private world was his solace from the horrors that appalled him. A refuge. A place to be. And now, that apocalyptic horror.

How could I make sense of things? So many letters unread. Some envelopes looked clearly official. Things official tend to be either boringly trivial or else frighteningly urgent. The pictures that had fallen from the walls had to go back to their hooks. But now their wall space was taken by oscillating towers of refuse. But was it really refuse? It was very hard to see. The scattered books, a great many, had to be gathered and put in some sort of order. But order required space. All space had been invaded. João appeared at the threshold of the door carrying an armful of notebooks. Alberto's poems and diaries. They absolutely needed to be rescued and kept safe. I had never read his diaries. Alberto had asked me to keep them away from the public eye for "at least" ten years after his death. I had to take them with me. But I thought it best to find them and gather them all together before taking them away from that disheartening scene. João took the notebooks to the most protected spot that he could find. Coming to the sitting room he nearly stepped on a painting half hidden under newspapers.

Trying to walk on that floor required both a keen eye and a keener sense of balance. A tip-toe and zigzag kind of dance. Miraculously, I stopped João. His foot was poised inches away from the surface of the canvas. It was a lovely oil painting. The artist was Jean Hugo. Alberto knew Jean Hugo from 52 Tite Street. He was married to Lauretta, a Hope-Nicholson daughter.

They lived an enchanted life, in Mas-de-Fourques, an old family farm, located in the south of France. Alberto visited them there. He came back with lovely souvenirs. Among them five portraits of himself by Jean Hugo. Jean was Victor Hugo's great-grandson. He painted miniature gouaches that were imbued with magnificence. Most of them were rural landscapes. Alberto showed them to me with pure pride and delight. I thought of Sienese painting when I saw them. Hugo's early life in Paris was shared with legendary members of a unique generation: Jean Cocteau, Erik Satie, Picasso, Paul Éluard, Colette, Blaise Cendrars. A magical circle of friends. It was through Jean Hugo that Alberto met the painters Vieira da Silva and her husband, Arpad Szenes. They lived in Paris and spent their summers in Yèvre-le-Chatêl. Alberto, who loved them both, visited them every year. They were equally fond of him and introduced him in turn to their own friends. Friends such as René Char, who inscribed one of his books to Alberto with the following words:

For Alberto de Lacerda / who knows./ His friend / René Char

With Arpad Szenes & Vieira da Silva, Loire, France, 1964.

With all these wonderful threads Alberto wove the surprisingly textured pattern of his life.

With Adolfo Cascais Monteiro, Waterloo Bridge, London, 1952.

João's assessment of the situation was more objective than mine. All the rubbish had to go. Yes, we were sifting for gold. But the rubbish had to go. All the rest had to be packed and kept safely somewhere. Another warehouse, most probably. Maybe the one where Alberto's things were kept. We left the flat and went there. It was surprisingly close. The manager came to see me and made a point of explaining that the internet had saved Alberto's unit from a radical clearing out. The irony of it all. Alberto hated the mere mention of the internet.

"You know?" he said, "Mr de Lacerda came here from time to time. He paid by cheque, often a post-dated cheque, went up to look at the unit, stayed up there a while and limped away. He did have a limp, didn't he? I can't imagine what he went to look at. Everything in there is kept in taped up boxes. Anyway, that's how it was. This is your total to pay. If you want to have a look, go right ahead. Here's the key. Just bring it back when you're finished. Payment is overdue. Just a reminder!"

João and I went up to look at the unit. It was full from top to bottom. The man had mentioned around two hundred boxes. I would have said more than that. Some of them bulged. They formed a compact block from wall to wall and all the way to the top. Leaning against the bottom row, there was quite a large art folder. We untied the top and sides and flipped it open. An enlarged photo appeared: Ravi Shankar. Autographed. We flipped that. Another photo: Mikhail Baryshnikov. Autographed. Another flip and yet another photo: Alberto. A much younger Alberto smiling a mischievous smile. It was a photo from his Austin period.

Austin remained for him a treasured memory. He loved the conviviality, the energy, the sense of space, the lovely weather. He wrote many poems there. One of those poems sums up his feelings most eloquently. It has no title and it consists of one word. One single word on the page.

Paradise

America saved Alberto from disaster. His freelance work as a writer was not enough to maintain him. The Austin job, a visiting professorship, was providential. But there was more than the climate and the sense of space and openness of the people, and the relief of a salary paid regularly every month, to give him a new lease on life. Beyond all the human warmth, the new friends, the creativity, he was inspired by the collective energy of the movements that were happening at the time: the anti-war movement, civil rights, gay rights, women's rights.

They all impassioned Alberto, whose sole obsession, in his own words, was freedom. His poetry, rich as it is in themes and tone, found a new register there, echoing the voices of protest that he heard.

El gran teatro del mundo

Vietnam
      Cambodia
           Life Magazine
                  Time Magazine
And TV
Images
      and more images
           and more and more images
Nothing exists
      I don't exist
        You don't exist
            He doesn't exist

We don't exist
You don't exist
They don't exist

Images exist
Mommy

More Vietnam (on television)
   more Cambodia (on TV)
More-communism-on-TV-more-anti-more hatred
   hatred is a virile reproductive force
Schlitz drink Schlitz in the U.S. Munich Bürgerbräukeller
Drink the well-paid piss of the C.I.A.
Long live the National Guard in a permanent state of copulation!
Down with mexicans, indians and jews! Down with negroes!
To kill is a true act, a virile act, a complete act!
(To die is shameful, although death doesn't really exist. Death is
the one universal triumph
Of the communist lie.)

To order killings is an act even more true more virile and more
   complete.
Step right up, gentlemen! Come and take a look at images, more
   images!
Anyone who's not a student, not a poet or a black won't have to
   pay a thing!
Come and see the Universal American Theater!
Come and see the moon invade Cambodia,
The moon—that work of genius by President Nixon
And the best American magazines!
The moon—right (not the left) breast of Shirley Temple,
Ronald Reagan and John Wayne!
Come and see Time magazine in a state of beatific erection,
Followed on the spot by instant total penetration of its
informative cock into the virile vulva of the North-American
   population!
Come and see the mystical union of the people and the press!
Come and see the perfect copulation! The ultimate couple!

Long live the most holy trinity of images:
Time magazine, the silent majority and TV
In color!

All in living color!

This poem was translated by Alberto's Austin friend Harriett Ann Watts. When Penguin Books published her translations of poems by Arp, Schwitters and Klee, Alberto bought various copies to present as special gifts. As a personal gift to Alberto, Harriett gave him the typescript of her book.

With Harriett Watts and friend, Austin, TX, 1968.

(Opposite page)
With Yves Bonnefoy & Jean Fanchette, Chelsea, London, 1961.)

I had very hard decisions to make in Primrose Mansions. Painful decisions to face. No one had been there in years. Beyond untidiness, Alberto's former ability to cope with his basic needs had simply left him. His acute sense of privacy prevented him from seeking any help. Offers were made. He rejected them outright. The loss of his telephone isolated him further.

His ancient record player stopped working. Someone gave him a portable CD player. He started buying CDs but barely used the machine. He never really liked it. Music ceased. The quality of his private life declined. He maintained his daily outings. But coming home in the evening became a bitter routine. He was completely alone. True to himself till the end, he wrote poems. More and more poems appeared everywhere.

Alberto's bedroom was the hardest room to see. Only the presence of the bed could justify describing it as the room where he slept. The bed was a battered raft amid flotsam, floating cargo. The whole room looked like a shipwreck. The bed itself consisted of a square wooden platform covering two enormous drawers. Both the platform and the drawers were purpose-built by a friend. They were built inside the room. An equally unusual mattress lay across the whole construction. The drawers were made as storage for his growing art collection. Alberto asked me one day to help him check what he had.

"I can't really remember everything that I've kept there. And you know, I love surprises."

Pulling those big drawers way out was a task that required powerful muscles and a solid back. They were boxes, more than drawers. None of the boxes had rollers and they were full to the brim. They were very hard to move. We pulled them only half way. They were full of works on paper. We looked at a few of those and then gave up. Alberto became quite pensive.

"I will simply have to find a larger home," he said.
And now it was my duty to take care of all of that. All of it and the contents of his unit in the warehouse.

João found more notebooks, a few large brown envelopes with manuscripts and also bundles of letters. Organized bundles, that is. We had gathered more than thirty notebooks. The letters, to my surprise, were separated by sender. The biggest bundle came from Edith Sitwell. In one of those letters, reacting to Alberto's book, his first, Edith Sitwell wrote: "…you are the real thing and it is precious rare."

Inside the brown envelopes there were also photographs. Alberto as a dapper young man. Alberto with friends. I was surprised to discover two or three taken by me. Alberto and Paula Rego on the Staten Island ferry. Alberto and the Brazilian poet Murilo Mendes in the West End. Alberto and the Portuguese poet Sophia de Mello Breyner. I remembered those occasions.

Memorable, all of them. There were also photographs of Alberto in different places with people I did not know. How could I ever discover who they were? Handwritten lists appeared. Some of those were quickly scribbled: lists of things to take on travel, shopping lists, reminders of things to buy, things to do. Other lists seemed more pondered. Lists of names. Illustrious names all seemingly unrelated. They only made sense to Alberto. There were also loose postcards. I noticed cards signed Umberto, Mary H., and Aunt Nora. Later inspection proved these names to belong to Umberto Morra, Bernard Berenson's assistant, Mary Hutchinson, the Bloomsbury party giver and arts patron, and Nora Wydenbruck, Rilke's translator and biographer, all of them writers in their own right. There were cards sent by Alberto to himself. No messages, just the cards. He mailed them as souvenirs of places where he had been, works of art that he admired. Cards sent fresh from experience to his future reminiscence. Two of those, identical oversize cards, showed a night view of the Thames by the Houses of Parliament. They were both addressed to William Shakespeare. The street address was given as 52 Tite Street. On one of those Alberto wrote Please do Not Bend.

36

As João brought me the notebooks I could not help leafing through Alberto's poems. For years, in person and over the phone, often during long transatlantic conversations, Alberto read me his poems, some of them only just finished, others rescued from forgetfulness or earlier moments of doubt. It was strange to read them there, after his death, in his flat. Leafing through pages at random, stopping on the shorter poems, I now felt strangely furtive, sneaky, almost disrespectful. Those poems were to be read in quite different circumstances, with proper appreciation, a tranquil sense of occasion. But I could not help myself and found poems such as these:

Words
        Interfere
                With reality
Above all
                With the reality
Of love

A number of them were untitled.

The streets continue
Their walk towards the sea

Darkness floats

A delightfully titled:

Motet

Orlando
Orlando di Lasso

Orlando
Oh Orlando
Di Lasso

Orlando di Lasso

Orlando
Di Lasso

Di Lasso

And the now poignantly appropriate:

Silence

Master

The supreme

Master

37

Paula Rego was kept informed of everything that was happening. Alberto and Paula were close friends for forty years. They looked forward to each other's company, went to exhibitions and the theatre together, and held each other in genuine admiration. They also inspired each other. Paula sought Alberto's advice, brought him gifts and drew his portrait. Alberto wrote about Paula and never lost an opportunity to praise and promote her work. The catalogue for Paula Rego's first solo exhibition, held in Lisbon, had a special introduction by Alberto. It was a poem. A prose poem. It was called 'Paula Rego'. The suggestiveness of Paula's themes, the strength and originality of her images, together with the literary references and political condemnation contained in Alberto's poem, brought a tremor to Lisbon's cultural world.

The dictator Salazar was then very much in power. The year was 1965. That same year Alberto published a new book of poems, *Opus 7*. He dedicated it to Paula. The last poem in that book is called 'A Poem Called Paula Rego'. That poem is the full version of the one published originally in Paula's catalogue. The news of Alberto's death came to her as both a shock and a loss.

Paula and Alberto shared friends and saw each other frequently. Paula and Victor Willing's home was Alberto's second home. But he loved inviting Paula on her own to Primrose Mansions. He played his records to her, introduced her to the work of various writers, and listened with great interest to her often disconcerting observations on matters of life and art. And above all he treasured the opportunity of conversing with her in Portuguese. He often called me at night to share these observations.

"Paula came here for dinner. We talked a great deal about Mantegna. Paula insisted that Bellini produces a sense of wonderment that is missing in Mantegna. But then she talked at length about an image by Mantegna that she described as 'a man looking into the abyss.' And she asked, 'Fear of hell?' I thought that I had seen that image. I went to check it just now and do you know what it is? Christ descending into limbo."

Alberto loved reading poems to Paula. He claimed that while he read "she listened with her whole being." And once, after she left, Alberto called me and said: "Paula was here for a wonderful couple of hours. We chatted incessantly, giggled, talked about the working practice of the poet and the painter. She says extraordinary things. Her responses are unique. When I die you have to tell her that I loved her from the bottom of my heart."

I did. When Alberto died.

38

The porters of Primrose Mansions warned me that the residents of the block "were fussing about that mess in number 48A." Alberto's unkempt appearance during his last few years and his secretive manner had raised a few eyebrows around the block. He looked shabby and furtive inside his old black parka, carrying that perpetual plastic bag. Everyone knew he had died. Could I do something about it? Any idea how long before the flat could be cleared? The concerns were not unreasonable. But a new preoccupation came to me. Did I really have the right to disturb Alberto's world? Even the ruins of his devastated world? Everything there had a story. Would the narrative be broken? Yet, the facts had to be faced. Alberto had to leave home.

I called the removal company that had moved us to Cascais. They had worked fast and well. I asked them to dispose of all the litter, and pack, remove, and store everything else in the flat. Everything minus the furniture. I wished to give it away. A date was promptly arranged for the company to start. And then John McEwen said that we should have photos taken of Alberto's home as we had found it. In spite of my growing need to protect Alberto's privacy, John's suggestion was not idle. I agreed. João, John, and Richard Roberts, a photographer friend of John's, came to the flat. Richard started right away to take photos here and there. The rest of us tried to salvage what we could. Then John asked me:

"Where did Alberto keep the rest of his works of art?"

I pointed to Alberto's bed. João helped us try to pull the two big boxes underneath. In vain. They felt glued to the floor. A layer of compacted paper under and in front of the boxes made it impossible to move them. Richard also tried to help. To no avail. And as we tried once again, all four of us, shoving, heaving, pulling hard, a rustling sound was heard. Something raced under the bed. Something dark and very fast. And then another. Mice. The flat had mice.

The thought of all of Alberto's work and correspondence and works of art being eaten by the mice gave us shivers. The clearing job was now extremely urgent. There was paper everywhere. All kinds of paper. A lot of it was support to works of art. João and I grabbed all of Alberto's notebooks and carried them to João's home.

39

Alberto was buried at the Brompton Cemetery. John took care of the arrangements. Alberto's friends were contacted and came to the gravesite. His dedicated former student and great personal friend Scott Laughlin came especially from California. Alberto's last visit to the United States had been to attend Scott's wedding. It would have meant a lot to Alberto to know that Scott was there. We had a simple, silent, but heartfelt ceremony by his grave. His coffin was descended into the ground and, one by one, we approached it with our thoughts. Handfuls of earth were thrown into the grave. Some flowers, too. There was a beautiful light. The day was pleasantly warm. Thinking of all our time together in museums, I threw a packet of demerara sugar into his grave. I went to fetch it at the National Gallery. Alberto called it "his home." Paula Rego's youngest daughter, the actress Victoria Willing, read one of Alberto's poems. It bears a title in Greek. Alberto told me that it means *The King of London*. The choice of Greek characters for the title is a device to keep the poem more private, and to place it on a level of classical timelessness. The theme is Alberto's love of London, "best loved of all cities."

Ο Του Λονδινίου Βασιλεύς

And also my free
Gladness
My weeping
My strength
My wonder
This is the land of the Dream
My most silent most difficult
Beloved friend
This is the river
Made of bombed houses
Of beautiful mysterious faces

Of the cockney vowels the immense palaces
The sombre quaysides
Very old wood
Swarms of gentle people
These are the tears
And also my joy
The grief of life finally accepted
My favourite form of inhabiting the world
My throne

River city
This is my city
This city is mine
Into the beloved the lover is transformed

My supreme majestic calm
Shakespearean forest
It embraces
Naturally everything

To this enchanted forest I came to be born
When I was twenty three

40

Paula made all the arrangements for Alberto's farewell party. It was held at his favourite restaurant under the Waterloo Bridge. The choice could not have been better. She took care of everything. It was Paula's party for Alberto. The wines and all the food were Portuguese.

Alberto was a great lover of Portuguese cuisine. He rated it third in the world following French and Chinese. Surprisingly, perhaps, he collected recipes. Inside those large brown envelopes that appeared in his flat, there were handwritten recipes and others torn out of magazines and newspapers. And he loved cookery books. He purchased hundreds of them for his own pleasure and also to give to friends. One day he brought me a copy of a richly illustrated book called *Dining with Picasso*. The author is Ermine Herscher. As he presented it to me he said: "I don't know anything about this lady, but I owe her the exquisite pleasure of dining with Picasso and Fernande, and Olga and Françoise and Jacqueline and their friends! Max Jacob, Braque, Apollinaire! Can you imagine having a meal with Picasso and Apollinaire?"

And after a little pause he added: "I am sure that they would love *"arroz de grelos com pastéis de bacalhau"*, don't you agree?" We laughed. *Arroz de grelos* and *pastéis de bacalhau* is a traditional Portuguese meal. It consists of rice cooked with turnip sprouts sautéed in olive oil with onion and garlic, and salt cod fishcakes. The fishcakes are made with a mixture of shredded cod, chopped up onion and parsley, and mashed potato. Alberto was extremely partial to those. He tried to make them himself, but his efforts were not met with great success. Something about the moulding of the mixture with the help of two soup spoons. He liked watching that step when done by others and enjoyed the frying noise of the cakes in the saucepan. He loved the Portuguese words pertaining to cooking procedures. Words such as "blonding," for browning.

"Blonding! What a wonderfully delicate and descriptive word... Blonding!"

Paula made sure that there were *pastéis de bacalhau* at his farewell. The restaurant staff excelled at serving the farewell gathering in honour of their old customer. They told me that Alberto sent them postcards from Lisbon when he was visiting there. Memories of Alberto were shared by all of us present. Alberto would have loved it all: the food, the company, and Paula's extremely generous hospitality. As we were leaving the restaurant, the manager, Mr Antunes, pointed to Alberto's table and said: "This, as you know, was where Mr Alberto de Lacerda liked to sit. We would very much like to have his picture on the wall, right there, right above his place, to help us all think of him. If you could find us something suitable to put there we would be extremely grateful."

And then he paused, tilted his head just a little, and asked: "Excuse me. We have been wondering. Do you mind telling us... what did Mr Alberto de Lacerda do?"

I was surprised by the question. "He was a writer, a poet," I replied. Mr Antunes smiled: "We thought so... But you see?... We never asked him. We did not want to intrude!"

A smiling photo of Alberto as well as his poem 'Ecstasy' are now framed above his table.

41

The removal company came. Two skips were set up outside Primrose Mansions. João and I were there, keen on overseeing the work and keeping the mice away. Alberto had a horror of mice. And now they were roaming the flat. No pest control service could be called. Everything had to be saved. But there were other concerns. Some pictures had not yet been found.

Among those there was a portrait of Virginia Woolf by Duncan Grant. Alberto had paid a lot for it. It was a pencil drawing that he had been unable to resist. He bought it over a long period of time, cheque by cheque, month by month, until he could finally bring it home. He loved its spontaneity and delicacy, the beautifully suggested introspective mood of the sitter. And he had a plan for it.

Visiting the Courtauld Galleries on a particularly pleasant afternoon, Alberto, who had been chatting animatedly about the Bloosmbury Group, turned to me all of a sudden and said: "I have a favour to ask you."

He looked unexpectedly serious.

"It has to do with my drawing of Virginia Woolf by Duncan Grant. You know the one I mean, don't you? I would like it to come here, to the Courtauld," he said. "If they will take it, that is." It was all a bit mysterious. He went on: "I would like you to remember this when I die."

"Don't be morbid, Alberto!"

He grabbed my forearm and went on: "Please remember this: when I die I would like you to present that drawing to the Courtauld Gallery in my name in memory of Edith Sitwell and Arthur Waley. These are the words that you have to remember: Bequeathed by Alberto de Lacerda in memory of Edith Sitwell and Arthur Waley."

The moment had become entirely solemn. Alberto's hand was still grabbing my forearm. His eyes demanded a promise. I made it.

"I will, Alberto."

And now, the place on the wall where I remembered having seen that beautiful drawing was empty. A heap of rubbish ready for the skips outside had been swept against that wall. Could the drawing have fallen behind there? What if the glass was broken? What if the drawing was ruined? What if the removal men were to inadvertently throw it in the skip? And what about those horrible mice? The recovery of the Virginia Woolf portrait became another source of anxiety. João found it. It was intact. And in due course it was presented to the Courtauld Institute.

The gift was appreciatively accepted and duly acknowledged. The official announcement read:

> *"The Courtauld is delighted to announce the gift of a portrait drawing by Duncan Grant bequeathed by the Portuguese poet Alberto de Lacerda (1928-2007) in memory of Edith Sitwell and Arthur Waley. [...] The drawing came into the collection as a portrait of the famous writer Virginia Woolf."*

And then, surprisingly, this:

> *"[...] whilst the attribution is plausible, there might be closer similarities with Woolf's sister, the painter Vanessa Bell. [...] The portrait makes a fine and purposeful addition to the Courtauld's outstanding collection of works by members of the Bloomsbury Group."*

42

My return ticket was up. I had to go back to Lisbon. João told me not to worry. He would oversee the work. But there were things to be done before I went. There was a legal process to be started before probate could be granted. And there was more. I wanted to have a stone placed over Alberto's grave. That proved to be a lengthy process. A certain period of time had to elapse before the stone could be laid. The placing itself raised a further issue: for some unfathomable reason it had to be laid flat on the ground rather than standing as I had intended. Then came all the unsuspected choices associated with gravestones.

I was reminded of being taken as a growing child to the gentleman's outfitters to be measured for a winter coat. I went with my grandmother. The choice of cloth was an interminable chore. In her Edwardian manner, my grandmother was not only particularly selective but literally indefatigable. The cloth could not be too heavy, not too thick, not likely to stain or crease too easily. The colour had to be appropriate for my age and for my size. The cut had to be classical but not an imitation of a garment for adults. And then, the same preoccupations with the lining. And the buttons. The whole project took care of an afternoon.

Choosing a stone for Alberto's grave raised similar issues. What colour: white, black, grey, veined marble, green? What kind of surface? Slithery, porous? How breakable, how resistant? And then, what type of lettering and with or without a border? And what about the colour of the letters? Black? White? Gold? I could imagine Alberto becoming frightfully impatient with it all, but one thing I knew for sure. I knew what the stone should say. Simply this: Alberto de Lacerda, poet, his dates and a short poem. The shortest: *paraíso*. Paradise being Alberto's eternal quest.

43

All the materials stored in the warehouse were apparently safe. Safe but unknown, unread, unseen, unattainable. Locked in a London warehouse. Boxed in Boston.

Boston did not offer Alberto the fulfilment that he had experienced in Austin. Yet, he was there for some 25 years. And Boston rewarded him. He encountered old friends there and made lasting new friendships. Octavio and Marie Jo Paz were there. Jorge Guillén was there. Elizabeth Bishop was there. Yves Bonnefoy was there. Roger Shattuck was there. Anne Sexton, too. Alberto loved Anne Sexton. Her death was deeply lamented by Alberto. She was very fond of him. The books that she inscribed to him show it well:

> *You are too much,* she wrote.
> And *You are you! Poet extraordinaire!*
> And *Hurry back! Last time I saw you we hugged on street corners at BU.*

Boston had music, museums, the extravagant delight of the Isabella Stewart Gardner Museum. Alberto's new friends were poets: Rosanna Warren, Michael Benedikt, Marc Wiedershien, Ruth Lepson, Kathleen Aguero, Richard Hoffman, Celia Gilbert, Tino Villanueva. And to Alberto's utter delight, one extraordinary prose writer. One of his most cherished students, the one who gave him his BU farewell party. "There may be moist eyes," warned Alberto. There were. Alberto's, some of the guests' and the beautiful almond eyes of his beautiful hostess, whose name he always pronounced as if describing a flavour: Jhumpa. Jhumpa Lahiri.

With Jhumpa Lahiri, Waterloo Bridge, London, 1999.

44

The removal men worked fast. The skips outside were getting full and João kept a good eye on what was thrown. There were takers for some pieces of furniture. Inside the flat, buried things came to the surface. Surprising findings. Discoveries. Alberto's extraordinary eye as a collector placed him in a special category. His instinct was celebratory, his nature was democratic. He favoured originality over fame, authenticity over virtuosity. The territory that he covered was landmarked by novelty and experience. And now, a lot of that was at risk. The packers were stacking boxes into the spaces that they cleared. From there they went into their enormous van. I asked the foreman: "What about those two big drawers that are stuck under the bed?"

"We'll do them last. We need to pack their contents. But we need to clear more space. There isn't much room in here."

It made absolute sense, but I feared for their contents. Alberto's black parka had been left on his bed, just as we found it. Casually there. Now the mice had got to it.

For one of my last London encounters with Alberto we planned to meet at the Royal Academy. Alberto was strict in matters of punctuality. I was a few minutes late. The grey weather would not help Alberto's mood. I rushed towards the entrance of the patio and there, sheltering from a gust of wind and a few sprinkles of rain into the dark cavity of his parka, was Alberto, progressing towards the entrance.

"Alberto!" I called.

He turned his head, peering from inside the hood. For one brief moment I had a glimpse of the monk Savonarola.

"Most dreadful weather," he complained. And we went in. And now his parka was destroyed.

I thought of Alberto's pride in having been able to gather all those things, those works of art that were so special to him, and felt something close to panic. A growing feeling of panic made more intense for knowing how much they really mattered to

Alberto. And now I had to return to Cascais fearing the hunger of those horrid mice.

45

Alberto came to Cascais not too long before he died. He came at the invitation of the local Mayor. The ever growing disorder in Primrose Mansions had led him to repeat from time to time that he needed to have a larger flat. But the search for more space had two requirements that Alberto could not meet: money and the mind-set to face a hellish move. Alberto did not have the first and could certainly not face the second. His decline started there. He gave up.

As soon as we moved to Portugal I started thinking of a possible solution to Alberto's situation. He was quite alone in London. As time went by he suffered greater discomfort. If I could persuade the Mayor of Cascais to receive the bulk of Alberto's vast estate and create a cultural centre in his name, his London flat would become immediately more manageable.

Additionally, this would enable him to make a gradual comeback to Portugal's cultural scene. His reputation was fading. He had been away too long. Cascais was flooded with light and leaned over a stupendous bay. There were old city walls, bougainvillea, palm trees, winding streets and a fast train to Lisbon. Alberto could retain his London flat, alleviate its confusion, and keep in touch with old friends and new admirers.

I had a successful precedent for my plans. Quite a few years before that, I had conspired with the Gulbenkian Foundation to have an exhibition of items from Alberto's personal collection at their recently inaugurated Modern Art Centre. What I proposed was a combination of documents and works of art. The collector and the poet. The Gulbenkian Foundation had dedicated a similar exhibition to the French poet Saint-John Perse and I grabbed on that idea right away. Why not Alberto? I had seen the Saint-John Perse show. I knew what I was proposing.

I plotted it all quite shamelessly behind Alberto's back. Not a single word of it was spilled. And then, I wrote him a letter, followed by a formal letter from the Gulbenkian Foundation and a telephone call from me. Alberto was predictably indignant.

"What kind of an idea is that? These are not museum pieces. These are my personal things. Besides, what does anyone care if I have a drawing by Arpad, which I have, or a painting by Zurbarán, which regrettably, I don't! What does it matter to the Gulbenkian Foundation if I corresponded with the Sitwells or with the Wizard of Oz? And what if I have photographs posing side-by-side with Hockney, or with Alicia Markova, or Robert Duncan, or Octavio Paz? Octavio *and* Marie Jo Paz, for that matter? And what if I have the first editions of all the books published by my poet friends? Do I have things? Yes, I do. Of course I do. And they are here with me, they are all part of my world. My private world."

He ranted and I explained. I explained as calmly as I could, that more than just showing his belongings, he would be sharing his own inspiring life with the public. A richly documented life. I mentioned Saint-John Perse whom he greatly admired. And I reminded Alberto that he had a lot of items that would be of great interest to the public. Alberto pondered that issue. He was beginning to yield.

Then he phoned in great anxiety over who would be selecting what, and issues like transportation, insurance and local handling of his things. I referred him once again to the Gulbenkian proposal. All of that was guaranteed. Then he was seized again by a new preoccupation.

"I can't live with the thought that I am doing this for vanity! These are the things that I love. My things are not a collection. They have to do with me because they reflect my passions, my interests, my souvenirs."

I assuaged him all the way. Other voices joined my own. And the exhibition was held. It was called: *Alberto de Lacerda – A Poet's World*. It was a real success and he enjoyed it immensely. The Foundation brought him over for the opening and duration of the show. Alberto went there every day. He loved to answer questions from the public, to tell his stories, to see young enthusiasts cross the threshold of his world and "dream a little."

With that in mind I approached the Mayor of Cascais. He had seen Alberto's exhibition. He listened to my suggestion and thought it worthy of a proper try. Kindly, he invited Alberto to Cascais.

46

Alberto appreciated the Mayor's invitation. He accepted it, however, with a measure of reluctance. He had a genuine yearning to see Lisbon again, the river Tagus, some old surviving friends. But he arrived without joy.

"This is the age of vulgarity," he said as he greeted me. "I'm anticipating horrors and I wanted to come here just once more."

And he added: "The monster that oppressed Portugal for so long, could not obscure the light. The light is essential purity. It gave us the strength we needed to survive the tyranny."

He was silent for a moment:

"The oppressor now is vulgarity."

He paused again. He was moved. And then he added: "I wanted to see this light once again." I tried to sound optimistic:

"Yes, and there are new things to see since your last visit, Alberto. And there's the Mayor, of course. We must see him tomorrow and discuss what he can do."

"What do you mean, he can do?"

"For you, I mean."

"Well... I will see him, of course. I want to thank him for his kind invitation. But I can't really see what he can do. For me? What can he do?"

I changed the subject. I knew that Alberto was not keen to discuss the real reason for the Mayor's invitation. He was not really sold on the idea of a space where all "his things" could be kept.

"You will be staying in a good hotel. I am sure that you'll like it," I said.

He did. It was a lovely building, a palatial summer residence, perched on the rocks overlooking Cascais bay. Alberto arrived in the evening. The sea was calm. Intense blue. His room was large and airy and well furnished. He was pleased. His mood was improving. He joked about the size of both his bed and his bath.

"Orgy size," he said. And laughed.

"What did you say to the Mayor about my sexual needs? He must think they are Gargantuan!" He was now pleased to be back. I was relieved.

47

The next few days went quite fast. Alberto's moods oscillated between buoyancy and depression. He was pleased to be offered a "museum," as he started calling it, but he privately resisted the idea.

"What is going to happen to my things? And what do they actually want? And who is going to be in charge?"

The Mayor had told Alberto that Cascais would not be making any kind of impositions. It was all up to him. But his mind was elsewhere. His whole past was coming back.

I accompanied Alberto throughout his entire stay. Taking advantage of his one and only absence to visit a friend in Lisbon, I had a chat with the Mayor. He and Alberto had got on rather well. Rather formally, but well. Alberto had impressed the Mayor. Our private chat was productive. A secret pact was sealed pending Alberto's approval.

And now it was time to go. Alberto had an afternoon flight. I took him to have lunch at a traditional restaurant. The regular customers were office workers, shop attendants, cab drivers, students, old pensioners, local people. The food was plentiful, tasty and brought in by a good natured waiter. The decoration and the whole environment were entirely Portuguese. Floating bits of conversation captured Alberto's attention. He loved it all and ate with satisfaction. After lunch Alberto asked me to walk around just a little. His mood was changing. He mentioned nearby streets that he knew from earlier days. He feared "horrendous changes" that might have "disfigured them." He said this and hailed a cab.

"Shall we go that way, Alberto?"

"No, no. Not now. It's late. Let us go straight to the airport."

We arrived with time to spare. We sat down to have a coffee, and then I revealed the pact that I had made with the Mayor.

"Alberto," I said, "think about it. This is what can be done. The Mayor will house your collection. You keep with you everything that you do not wish to part with. The bulk of

104

your collection will be on loan to Cascais. They will offer you a contract. The idea is that Cascais will eventually inherit what you put there on display. Meanwhile, I have arranged for you to have a *pied à terre* at your disposal. In Cascais, of course. Close to your things and to us. You will be free to come and go as you please. The Mayor has also accepted to provide you with house cleaning. He will also give you a stipend to help you with your travelling costs. This will enable you to sort out your flat in London and to spend some time in Portugal. Your collection will be safe and you can visit your friends. Just think about it, Alberto."

He said nothing for a while. He got up to check his flight, dragging all his things with him. He kept his eyes on the board for quite a while and asked me if I had time to have yet another coffee. I did, of course, and we sat down once again, in a corner of his choosing. He repeated his routine of the positioning of a couple of chairs to lay his parka, his plastic bag, his accoutrements. He kept stirring his coffee and then, finally, he replied: "I'm tired. I'm really tired, you know? This trip has stirred old emotions... You have thought of everything. The Mayor was most hospitable. I am sincerely grateful. But you see?... I live in London!"

48

More boxes kept being marched out of Alberto's flat into the cavernous trucks parked in Prince of Wales Drive. I was amazed at the growing number of boxes leaving Primrose Mansions. The Boston boxes in the warehouse were left untouched. I realized that I was now committed to maintain two storage places full of items largely unknown to me. And now I had to fly back to Portugal. How could I catalogue them piece by piece? And where could they all be kept? And what about the mice in the flat? So much paper. So much that could be destroyed. I had to find a solution. The inheritance process had just been started in London. I could not even imagine when and how and in what country I could start dealing with Alberto's vast estate. His flat was still far from empty. The company employed to clear it was headquartered in Rye. That's where those boxes were going. Hundreds of boxes full of treasures unseen. Boxes and boxes in London, and now more boxes in Rye. There were plenty of decisions to be taken. Different footpaths to follow. Footprints from Alberto's grave.

Tombeau de Bill Evans

Footprints

Footprints left by someone
With bleeding feet

49

I took the plane back to Lisbon full of a sense of anxiety and growing responsibility. I had always assumed that Alberto had simply wanted me to be his literary executor. But now my duties had grown. His life was left in my hands. A life intensely lived and now needing validation. So much of it left untold. I could hear Alberto's voice telling me that no one cared, that distance erases all, that silence breeds forgetfulness. Throughout his life he often, and often poignantly, wrote about loss, and sadness and solitude but his legacy was the opposite of all that. His poetry above all was celebratory.

I wanted to bring him back as someone who had experienced what he described as a sense of glory. These are Alberto's own words:

> *The sense of glory. Nobody can take away from me the sense of glory – as Henry James and Herbert Read conceived it – of so, so many moments in my life. In spite of one thousand atrocities and injustices, in spite of all kinds of suffering, I have been able to reach the inner bliss of feeling at the centre of time, at the centre of space.*
>
> *Enchantment. The absolute. The ecstasy. In love, in eroticism, in nature, in friendship, in the aesthetic exper-ience, both as creator and spectator. Glory. An authentic sense of glory that fills me with tears and makes me kneel before eternity. Fonteyn was one of those miraculous beings who, almost every time I saw her dance (and it must have been hundreds of times) has brought me to that indescribable, that incomparable centre. Certain music of Tchaikovsky, the great Petipa ballets, the countless pieces choreographed by Balanchine, evoke that sense of wonderment. It is an absolute sensation, concrete but generous to the absolute (an iridescence) that is impossible to describe.*

Lisbon was visible now. The plane was landing. Domes looming up, tiled roofs, the splendid sight of the river. I wanted to be with Mary and our son. I felt hopeful. We were now being instructed to be ready for our landing. A poem came to my mind:

And suddenly an angel
Descends
Upon the convulsive knot

Blue matter

Alberto wrote it, of course.

50

As soon as I returned to Portugal I initiated contacts to have his estate properly installed as a combined gallery, library, and research centre. The grant of probate was eventually issued. I could finally start working on all that Alberto had left me.

But for me, a fundamental question still remained. What was materially there in Alberto's vast estate and what could I do with it all? An idea came to me. During Alberto's last trip to Lisbon, I had brought him to see former President Mário Soares. After his last mandate, an institution similar to an American presidential library was created. It is called the Mário Soares Foundation. It stands opposite the national Parliament.

During Alberto's last visit, Mário Soares received him there with great courtesy. As a life-long lover of literature he had just published a selection of his favourite poems by his favourite poets. Alberto was represented in that book. Mário Soares made a point of offering an autographed copy of his personal anthology to Alberto. He talked a little about it, he inscribed it to Alberto and before he handed it to him, he started reading aloud. He read Alberto's own 'Ode to the Tagus'. He read it extremely well and with contained emotion. Alberto was close to tears. So was I. It was a privileged moment to see those two extraordinary men connected by the experience of a poem. Alberto's poem.

My first efforts to take care of the estate in Cascais were not successful. Everything had remained in two different English cities, in two separate warehouses and in conditions that, in the long range, I deemed unsafe. All those books, and papers, and works of art were packed for transportation, not for storage. Besides my preoccupation with conservation issues I still had no way of knowing what was kept inside those hundreds and hundreds of taped cardboard boxes.

Besides the collector's instinct that guided his acquisitions, Alberto's passionate nature, his sense of humour, his love of originality, his curiosity, his taste, required all those boxes to be opened. Everything had to be adequately stored and properly conserved. No solution was in sight. And then a thought came to me. I went to see Mário Soares, hoping that he would help me with a word of guidance, a useful contact. He gave me a princely reply: "Bring it all here," he said. "If you trust us, we will receive it, clean it, sort it, catalogue it. You will help us clarify anything that has to do with Alberto's life and works. As you know we are a foundation. We receive money for projects. Alberto de Lacerda will be our next project. The estate remains entirely in your hands. You will decide how to use it. We will simply make sure that it is rescued and treated."

It was. It took three years.

Two huge trucks arrived at the Mário Soares Foundation. The total weight of the cargo was an incredible 16 tons. It filled every bit of space that could be found in the building. Everyone there was astounded. When the cleaning and the sorting and the numbering of the specimens was completed there were approximately: 21,000 books and publications; 9,000 LP recordings; 13,000 literary documents; 12,000 photographs; and close to 1,000 works of art. Other items still turned up as time progressed. Mercifully, the mice had not touched a single poem, a single book, a single work of art. Their gluttony was confined to newsprint.

The bulk of Alberto's estate has now been donated to the National Library of Portugal. His prodigious collection of LPs has been donated to the Archive of the Mário Soares Foundation where its detailed cataloguing was in progress.

My attempts to create Alberto's centre were not successful. Impediments intervened. Yet, Alberto's memory is being honoured. Events in Boston, Lisbon, and New York have taken place. Exhibitions and poetry readings have been held. Books and catalogues have been published. His work has had new translations. Works of art have been loaned. The celebration continues.

This is an unpublished poem:

the indifference of successive doors

the stairway

Oxford,
November 2014

Alberto's sitting-room, 2007. Photo by Richard Roberts.

In Green Park, London, 1980s.

Lightning Source UK Ltd.
Milton Keynes UK
UKHW010913150222
398720UK00001B/234

9 781848 613638